châteaux of the Loire

châteaux of the Loire

Text by Sabine Melchior-Bonnet

translation
by Angela Armstrong

LIBRAIRIE LAROUSSE
17, rue du Montparnasse, Paris

Iconography: C. Champougny
Proof-reading: B. Dauphin and C. Brami
Art directors: F. Longuépée and H. Serres-Cousiné
Editorial office: M.-S. Gossot
Lay-out: J. Cousiño

Larousse ISBN 2-03-523106-X
Newnes ISBN 0-600-35788-0

The château d'Amboise dominates the town 'which seems to lie at its foot like a pile of little pebbles' (Flaubert). All the grace and splendour of the Val de Loire are inscribed in this majestic edifice with its towers, turrets and rooftops, at the foot of which winds the Loire.

CHAMBORD, BLOIS, CHAUMONT, AMBOISE, Chenonceaux, Azay-le-Rideau, Langeais, Ussé: a royal itinerary overflowing with art and history. Within a rectangular area 250 by 100 kilometres, situated between Gien and Angers, Orléans and Loches, France possesses an unequalled concentration of riches. For nearly two centuries, from 1418 to 1588, this was the scene for some of the most important events in French history.

These châteaux, linked to the art of the court, were built to impress, to be seen from a long way off. They had to reflect the glory of a prince or great lord and herald his greatness; and greatness is measured by the extravangance of expense. Several times each year the Valois retinue wended its way from one château to another, with its long straggling lines of decked horses, cartloads of tapestries and trestle tables, attendant pages and nobles dressed in costumes sparkling with gold. What a dazzling sight moving slowly along the river bank! The king was on show before his cheering subjects and his journey was a display of strength, as were his châteaux.

Nowadays, processions of a different kind flock to these magnificent gems, now empty of their kings, time-pressed tourists anxious to pack four, six or even ten châteaux into one day - admiration always needs to set records! Behind the guide they learn to

identify the monogram of each owner: the porcupine of Louis XII, the Franciscan girdle of Anne of Brittany and the intertwined initials of Henry II and Diane de Poitiers. Through *sons et lumières* entertainments the tourist can relive bygone feasts, and discover the incredible display with which the kings used to impress their subjects.

Honour to whom honour is due: before crossing the threshold of these châteaux, let us salute their royal hosts: Charles VIII, Louis XII and François I.

The royal emblems are like their signatures.

The royal suite : the tinkling of armour and trampling of horses' hooves resound along the roads of the Val de Loire when the king moves from one château to another; the tents which accommodate the court, have barely been taken down, but already thousands of guards and courtiers precede the palanquin of Catherine de Medicis.

On their return from the Italian wars the Valois family took a dislike to their gloomy towers. They wanted to let in light, they pierced the walls, transformed moats into gardens, constructed terraces and galleries where the court could parade and put itself on show. Nothing was too good for the king and his retinue of gentlemen avid for honour and riches. Financiers haggled with creditors and loans; public offices were put up for sale; silverware was melted down and the treasury almost touched rock bottom. But no matter! As a result of their wild lavishness all along the banks of the Loire the châteaux remain, which Balzac so attractively described as 'the signs of royal benevolence'.

To talk of 'royal benevolence' is going too far. This lavish decor cut out of the white Bourré stone certainly provided a setting for balls and romances: here the Duchess of Brittany was married, there the young ladies of the Flying Squadron danced the *volte* and the *branle*. But it also provided the background for countless plots and betrayals beneath flickering torchlight, innumerable scenes of assassination and debauchery with corpses lying rotting on the balconies...

Could these distinguished, sometimes tragic settings for the Renaissance have been erected anywhere but on the banks of the Loire, anywhere than in this garden of France cherished by Rabelais? Undoubtedly, Gaillon in the Eure and Anet in Eure-et-Loir give the lie to this. But nowhere else could they have found such a combination of rich lands, and light and water of an almost Italian delicacy. Water, the mirror of beauty, pervades the scene: the waters of the Loire flowing between willows and poplars, swollen by its tributaries, the Beuvron, Cher, Indre, Vienne and Loir. It forms a labyrinth of sleepy riverlets spangled with water lilies, lingering among reedy banks and washing the foot of a turret. The river, like Ariadne's thread, guides the visitor from one château to another, lets him discover; beside the pompous monuments of history, a manor house with blue slated roofs, a dovecote in the Sologne, a little country residence with its crest and climbing rose bushes. This is truly 'doulce France', beloved by Ronsard, Du Bellay, Rabelais and Balzac, a land of refined civilization where the art of living was cultivated to a greater height than elsewhere. □

a river civilization

IF KINGS HAVE OFFERED the Loire its decoration of castles, in exchange the Loire has well served its kings. The Loire was a royal waterway for many kinds of barges, *galiotes*, *gabares* and *chalandoux*; let the current carry us lazily along. The Loire boatmen were experts at making their way between the banks of golden sand. This was how the Valois princes travelled in their decorated boats. Anne of Brittany owned her own barge which enabled her to travel from Tours to Amboise and even as far as Nantes whenever she wished.

The Touraine and Blésois regions owe their thriving activity to the Loire and, but for the river, there would have been no castles. Forming a strategic frontier, a gateway to the region, the river constitued a vital pipeline providing the heartlands of France with men and merchandise, its rich alluvial deposits fertilizing the land and feeding the rich pastures. The Valois family would, no doubt, no longer recognize in today's golden wheat fields and neat patchwork of cultivated land, the exuberant, undisciplined countryside which still existed in the 16th century. At that time, dense forests covered the entire plain between the Loire and its tributary, the Loir, populated by wolves, boars and deer, while otters and minks made their homes along the banks of the Sologne rivers. However, even then, the plough-shares gradually ate into the large expanses abounding with game and the red marshlands, which cause Ronsard to lament: 'O woodcutter, stop your work...'

Since the beginning of time, kings and great lords have had a passion for hunting; chasing the stag they forgot wars and the cares of state. It is not surprising that the Valois, like the Capetian family, were attract-

In April or May, swollen by the alluvial waters from the Auvergne mountains, the magnificent Loire takes on the appearance of a big lake (at Chaingy, Loiret).

ed to these immense wooded lands lying so close to the fertile plains of the Beauce.

Since the 12th century, the grape-vine had been firmly established along the bank of the Loire, with its well exposed slopes, temperate climate and rich soil, and the vineyards continued to spread under the attentive care of the large abbeys and noble households. At that time cellars, wine presses and winegrowers'houses spread all over the hills, a region of settlement. The humblest dwelling was covered with trellises: it is the vine that makes the Touraine inhabitants mischievous, so they say. Nature has generously provided cellars. The tender white chalk of the Touraine was dug out like soft cheese and provided cool resting places for the barrels and casks. White, red and *rosé* wine: something for everyone's taste. Ronsard appreciated the wine of Anjou, and Rabelais the delicate white of Touraine. Wine cheers the saddened heart and was used in the preparation of medicines; and, according to Charles d'Orléans, these wines are unsurpassed anywhere in France: the Flemish, Picards and English bought them up by the cartload.

With game, wine and wheat, there was enough to satisfy even the most demanding of princes. The rivers provided an abundance of fish, such as trout, lampreys, salmon and pike and the sea was only a few days sailing away. But above all, a climate so mild that one can live to be a hundred encourages the cultivation of the most delicate fruits and vegetables. 'A land of sweetness, happiness and delight', cries Tasso. Dating back to the reign of Louis XI, the villages of the Indre, Vienne and Cher have been flowered orchards, whose fruits, like the well-known pears called *bon-chrétien*, remind one of the fruits of paradise. However, the introduction of the rarest species is due to Charles

The 16th century discovered the art of gardens. Ornamental foliage, beds of box and yew trees, patches of vegetables, the scent of pot herbs; each year the gardeners of Villandry planted over 60,000 flowers and as many vegetables in a garden a hectare in size.

On the sunlit slopes, the vineyard stretches out in regular lines. Wines from Anjou, Chinon, Bourgueil, Vouvray, Montlouis, are so varied that there is a different one to accompany every dish.

The earliest palaces of our ancestors! The chalky cliffs of the Loire are riddled with troglodyte dwellings like rabbit warrens. Some of them are still inhabited, but the majority have been transformed into cellars where the wines of Touraine slowly come to maturity.

VII on his return from Italy. With the aid of Italian gardeners, each château had its vegetable garden spread out like an embroidered carpet, planted with pumpkins, tomatoes, melons and cucumbers. Each lord had to have his garden and Ronsard was more than proud of his vegetable patch sown with 'artichokes, lettuce, asparagus, pumpkins and vegetable marrows from Touraine'. He even offered Charles IX melons, so perfumed that he deemed them worthy of a king. Langeais included three melons in his coat of arms; and after all, a French queen, Claude, gave her name to a particular kind of plum.

Bustling activity

What bustling activity along the riverside! So long as roads were no more than goat tracks, the Loire remained a privileged means of transport. In Roman times, the Cher and the Loire were used to get from Bourgogne to the Atlantic. Charles d'Orléans liked to leave his château at Blois on the Loire banks and watch the boats sailing by. A poetical exaggeration? As for La Fontaine, he considered Orléans 'like the port of Constantinople in miniature'. During the Ancien Régime, the river was the principal ordinary way from Paris to Nantes. Mme de Sévigné took a coach to Orléans, where twenty bargemen pressed their services on her and, in less than three days she arrived at her destination, delighted with the journey. However, it was wise to follow the advice of this inhabitant of Strasbourg, who spoke from experience '1) You must first inspect the boat to make sure it is seaworthy; 2) Do not give any money to the bargee, but stipulate in your contract that he will be paid on arrival; 3) Specifically lay down that the owner remains on the boat, otherwise they travel for a few leagues with you then leave you with young inexperienced men, etc.' When

Nowadays the Loire is a sleepy river, but for centuries it was the scene of intense activity, dotted with square white sails which glided up the river transporting their precious cargoes as far as Orléans.

the Briare canal was completed in 1642, linking Briare to Montargis, the river traffic doubled in importance. In 1829, the first steam ship came up as far as Orléans and the Orléans-Nantes service, which took two days, caused a sensation. However, competition from the rail service from Orléans led to the decline of the Loire and the river silted up.

There is no doubt about the river's changeable nature. The upper course, rushing down from the Auvergne mountains, is untamable, gouging out its course in the impervious rocks. Only from Roanne does it become navigable. The Loire of the châteaux begins at Gien: the banks widen out, push back the embankments of the Sologne and forest greenery of Orléans. The river then meanders in wide loops between embankments built in the 12th century for kilometres to correct its irregular course; a weak and flimsy protection soon broken down by the river swollen with rain and melting snow. The violence of these devastating floods is well-known to the inhabitants of the Loire.

But the changeable nature of the Loire did not make navigation impossible. On balmy summer days, when the river is reduced to no more than a thin trickle of water amidst the sand, the boatmen hauled up their craft on the beach, then down again a few kilometres further on; however, since the Middle Ages, men have been employed to dredge the silted passageways. The Loire barge called *gabare* was a flat-bottomed boat which only needed one metre of draught to carry a hundred tons. For three or four centuries its construction remained almost unchanged, made of oak, twenty metres in length, it floated easily down the river and thanks to the west wind, called the *galerne*, came up with almost as much ease. When the wind died down the sailors would take a drink at the inn and spin yarns. With a good wind filling the sails, they would rush onto the deck of, the barge taking the lead, followed by several other smaller craft laden with precious goods for the court: silks from Lyon and Milan, oil from Provence, cloth from Malines, iron from Spain and even local products such as quince preserves from Orléans (jelly made from apples and quinces), salmon, oysters, salt, wheat. The navigation period was short, and they took advantage of it by sailing one behind the other, hull against hull.

Sailors and merchants grouped together in a powerful association, 'the Corporation of merchants using the Loire river and other rivers which flow into it'. From the Middle Ages it enjoyed royal protection and its purpose was to support the humblest of barge men on condition he had paid his subscription. It also kept an eye on the state of the navigable channels, canals, toll taxes, the condition of lock-gates: Louis XI had, in fact, ordered the extension of the embankment as far as Tours. The river was divided into sections and at each section the corporation checked that the lord who collected the toll fees fulfilled his engagements; moveable mills were not to hinder traffic and the embankments were to be kept in good condition.

There were numerous tolls: in 1518, as many as two hundred on the Loire and its tributaries, but the same tariffs did not apply to all merchants; for the local people they were lower than for foreigners. The economic role of the Loire can be estimated by the number of money changers: seventy-nine, out of seven hundred and fifty in France, lived along the middle section of the Loire. Tours and Orléans were noted as warehouses for all kinds of products.

From bourgeois to lord of the manor

Commerce provided a source of wealth; the towns were filled with superbly built houses. The Groslot family, master leather dealers at Orléans around 1450, are a good example of a bourgeois family who rose in the social scale after making their fortune in commerce. The second generation was able to study at the university of Orléans and the third, Jacques Groslot, became a magistrate and counsellor to the king and chancellor to the Queen of Navarre (he supported the Reformation). He made a good marriage and around 1531, had made enough money to build a small château outside the town. A patent letter from François I even authorized him to build a drawbridge 'provided it is detrimental to no one'. He was then only one step away from adding a wing and a tower to the main building, renting out his lands and obtaining the right to be lord of the manor.

There is no doubt that the establishment of the Valois court in the valley of the Loire gave impetus to this kind of social ascension. In the wake of the court, fortunes were made and sometimes lost. The Doucet, Robertet, Briçonnet, Bohier and Hurault families, and many others, are examples of success through official position and wealth, which a network of alliances and well-made marriages consolidated. Later on we shall take a look at their châteaux.

A retinue of artists and craftsmen followed in the wake of the king. The Valois family encouraged everything which satisfied their appetite for luxury and

Besides the historical châteaux the Touraine is sown with fortified farms and gentilhommières. *Around a bend, the delighted traveller comes across delicately sculptured windows, an elegant main building, a turret beside a vegetable garden, vestiges of the age of the Renaissance.*

beauty. Tapestry workshops followed in the steps of the court along the Loire; they were established at Tours under Louis XI, at Angers under Charles VIII, and at Blois under Louis XII. The paper industry, the handmaiden of Humanism, developed at Meung-sur-Loire and it is known that Christophe Plantin who settled at Anvers came from the Touraine. In 1553 an edict by Henry II exempted from taxes 'all printed matter, bound or unbound'. Tours owes its silk manufactures to Louis XI: silk weavers were imported from Lyon and Milan, which enabled Jean Briçonnet to exhibit gold cloth of first-class quality in London. The industry became so prosperous that its plush, taffeta and velvet was exported to Spain and even Italy in the 17th century.

With its crenellated towers rising out of the mist, its fairy-like palaces reflected in pools of water, its festivities and wealth, was the valley of the Loire an earthly

The joy of harvest time : this Flemish tapestry pictures one of the most important scenes of country life in the Val de Loire. The winegrowers cut down the grapes which are laid in baskets and handed to wine-pressers. The first pressing produces a liquid called the mère goutte, *which is the most appreciated wine.*

paradise? The Wars of Religion divided the inhabitants and led to murder on both sides. A terrible plague spread down the river in 1583, 1584 and again in 1598. It was responsible for the death of a part of the population of Tours in 1607; the nobles remained entrenched in their castles. Famine and bitter winters caused havoc in the 17th century. Even the splendour and luxury of court life had its reverse side: nobles ruined themselves to keep up to the standards set by the court, bankruptcy followed bankruptcy. As soon as the Valois forsook the Loire, the survival of commerce and industry was put in jeopardy through lack of customers. Even winegrowers had to abandon first-class vineyards for the same reason. Grandeur and decadence... □

The first book printed in the Val de Loire was produced by a press at Orléans in 1481. The number of copies printed then cannot be compared with present day editions : at that time a thousand copies was considered a best-seller! In 1526, the library of the château de Blois included 2,000 books, and fifteen years later, 16,000.

from castle to castle: a quick history

Plessis-Bourré is a sort of model château : its lay-out, a rectangular mass with towers at each corner, with one high and three low wings, was copied all over France. Jean Bourré, treasurer to Louis XI and owner, started building in 1468, after having completed work on Langeais.

LIKE FLAUBERT DREAMING before the crimson canopied bed of Diane de Poitiers at Chenonceaux, let us make a digression: if only these famous portraits hanging on the castle walls would leave their gilded frames and relate their adventures, tell us about their tastes, passions and misfortunes and what their life was like! But they remain silent beneath the age-old dust. And Flaubert, who travelled up and down the Loire with his insatiable curiosity admitted his disappointment: 'it is an irritating and fascinating curiosity, a dreaming desire to know, like one has for the unknown past of a mistress...'

Without man, the most beautiful monuments and the most splendid halls are nothing more than empty shells. One must keep the company of princes in order to understand their palaces and know their palaces to detect the secrets of princes. To wander through the châteaux of the Loire is to let history and its memories flow back to the surface like the blood of life.

Checkmate to the king

Two o'clock in the morning on 29 May 1418: the Burgundians throng into Paris through the gate of Saint-Germain and start to plunder and loot. The Dauphin of France, Charles, aged 16, takes refuge in the Bastille, but the fighting between the Armagnacs and Burgundians takes such a violent turn that his life is in danger. That night a devoted old gentleman wraps the young man in warm clothes and carries

The château de Mehun-sur-Yèvre where the young Charles VII took refuge, belonged to the Duc de Berry, which is why it is included in the miniature from the Très riches Heures. *The austerity of the base contrasts with the marvellous decoration of the superstructures.*

him off on horseback to Bourges along the Melun road. Here he is welcomed by his uncle, Jean de Berry, in his castle filled with a collection of art treasures. This then was how the golden age of the châteaux of the Loire began, with a flight from fear.

Four years later, Charles VI, worn out by fits of madness, passed away and his son, the young Charles VII, was proclaimed king at Mehun-sur-Yèvre. At that time he was no more than the little king of Bourges, without greatness, land or prestige. When he arrived on the banks of the Loire, only his Duchy of Touraine was under his control. But with the support of two impregnable fortresses, Loches and Chinon, he was to conquer his kingdom town by town. Twenty years later, he made a triumphal entry into Paris, but refused to reside there. Charles loved the Val de Loire and became the first king of Touraine; a nomadic king, constantly on the move with his little retinue of favourites from Chinon to Loches, Loches to Tours, Tours to Mehun-sur-Yèvre.

His successors were to do the same. Louis XI and Charles VIII could have returned to live in the Capetian capital, but they also preferred to reside on the banks of the Loire. The result was that for a hundred and seventy years the main events of French political life took place between Orléans and Angers. The protracted stay of the sovereigns and the prosperity which accompanied peace led to a blooming of turrets in the following years.

The Val de Loire had not waited for Charles VII to become a country of châteaux. For over five centuries sturdy towers had been firmly planted in the soil; ever since the powerful counts of Anjou had quarelled with the no less powerful counts of Blois over the rich lands of Touraine. The feudal system of domains had led to war, one domain against another, each side trying to quench its thirst for land by fighting-fights between great barons or ferocious animals, which more often than not resembled bandit raids rather than war.

Around the year 1000, there was continual fighting between the Caesar of Anjou, Fulk Nerra and Thibaud the Deceiver or his successor, Eudes de Blois. Each one firmly placed his fortress at the limits of his conquests, marking his terrority or defending its access. Of Fulk Nerra, known as the Black Falcon, it was said that his

castles were as numerous as the days in a year. The heart of France was like a chessboard where two camps played in turn: checkmate to the king, the great loser in these battles! At first, the towers were wooden constructions set on embankments, then they became square-shaped stone fortresses overlooking the countryside: Langeais, Beaugency, Montrichard, Montbazon and so many others... During the 13th and 14th centuries the art of war evolves: to make their assault more difficult the towers become rounded, widen out at the base and the summits are topped with crenellations, machicolations, *chemin de ronde* from which boiling oil can be thrown over the assailants. The curtain wall, an extra protection, shelters the main building and the towers are crowned with numerous defensive levels.

From safety to comfort

One of the greatest merits of the Capetian kings was to have brought the rebel strongholds of the great feudal lords to obedience. At the end of the 12th century, Philippe-Auguste snatched Anjou, Poitou, and Touraine from the hands of the Plantagenets, then kings of England, and the Valois inherited a powerful and magnificent kingdom.

However, as a result of inheritance laws and apanage — land given to younger sons — the crown had some difficulty in maintaining its unity. France continued to be divided into factions, the feudal system was restored and the English arrived in full force: the achievement of the Capetian kings had to be started again.

The treaty which terminated the Hundred Years War and the gradual pacification of the kingdom put an end to the mourning for the dead, the misery and the innumerable sieges. All these fortresses, armed and built for military purposes became

Fougères is a very old fortress, rebuilt under Louis XI by Pierre de Refuge. In spite of the medieval appearance of its buildings and square keep, the inner courtyard and its galleries with depressed arches recalls the Charles d'Orléans wing at the château de Blois.

Here at Chaumont, one can see the external paraphernalia of a fortified castle. The twin towers form a section cut on the southeastern front, behind a double drawbridge, one for foot passengers and one for carts. But the walls pierced with casement windows, the decorative freize, the parapet walk with its machicolations carved with the monograms of Diane de Poitiers contradict its military appearance.

useless, only suitable for housing prisoners within their grim walls. Building started once more with the notion that life was to be enjoyed and for the first time a preoccupation with comfort was added to that of security. Loop-holes were converted into windows, the proper residential building became independent of the military section, the castle was no longer a strong-hold but rather a fortified palace, square in shape with four large towers, including a wing with a high vaulted hall as became the lord's lifestyle: such a plan can be found at Langeais for example.

The next stage took place under Louis XI when a taste for decoration took precedence over the necessity for protection. Of course the building retained its defensive aspect with moats and drawbridges, usually with one tower higher than the others — a reminder of the old keep — but the three remaining wings of the quadrangle were low buildings; the windows were glazed and all kinds of Gothic features ornamented the crenellations and dormer windows. This type of design, that of Plessis-Bourré near Angers, was copied almost everywhere towards the end of the 15th century at Verger, Coudray-Montpensier, Montreuil-Bellay. It was, in fact to influence château architecture for nearly two centuries, in cases where the inner courtyard was enclosed by the construction of a low wing.

But at almost the same time, inventive architects were renewing the art of building and erecting the first manor houses.

The castles move down to the plain

It is not at all surprising that the new fashion of manor houses was first established in Anjou in the 15th century, in the province of the good King René, a lover of letters and good living: this patron of the arts and artists had no trace of the conquering fury of the old counts of Anjou. He was already part of the Renaissance, perhaps because of his Italian connections. Forsaking the large fortified castle, he had delightful residences built nearby, set in the heart of agricultural estates: Launay near Saumur, Reculée and Chanzé near Angers. 'Lying close the meadows', as Ronsard would say, these manor houses leave the rocky outcrops and hill tops, the better to appreciate pleasures of living and the well-known temperate climate of Anjou.

The new fashion was too attractive not to be copied and a taste for luxury is contagious. In Touraine, a poet-prince, cousin to René of Anjou, Charles d'Orléans, made innovations at Blois on his return from captivity: away with dark prisons and thick-walled masonry, make room for sun and light which can warm the apartments through arcaded galleries turned into promenades. Louis XI had similar ideas when he redecorated Plessis-lès-Tours. It is a simple, comfortable building, a country retreat, with a polychrome decoration of intertwined brick and stone. It was to become a model for a brick architecture which was widespread in Touraine at the end of the 15th century, at Luynes, Nançay, the château du Moulin de Lassay, Herbault...

The masons, with much taste and skill, endlessly varied the decoration using the different materials disposed in lozenges and black and red squares; the walls lost their thickness and were pierced with vast

Polychrome decoration of the château du Moulin at Lassay. The ornamentation of black lozenges on a red brick background which can be seen on the turret in the background, is very common in the Blésois region.

The grace of Italy harmonizing with the French gothic style : these mullioned windows look out over the parapet walk of the François I wing of the château de Blois. The pediments with niches decorated with shells and little angels are of Italian inspiration.

mullioned windows. If the castles still stood within moats and curves of the river, it was for the freshness of the water and the reflections of the sky. The military aspect had become no more than a decorative piece of fantasy, a charming illusion.

Perhaps the great empty halls one visits today seem icy and soulless? Nothing could have been less true at that time. Along the high walls in between the fireplace and windows, tapestries glowing with colours were hung: the court was still nomadic, it camped within the castle walls and carried off in chests those woollen partitions which servants used to attach to iron or wooden hooks, marking out an area, lining a doorway, arranging a cosy tent or providing the canopy or curtains for a bed. How good it was, during the cold winter months to be in this comfortable 'closet' or cabinet hung with tapestries in front of a tall fireplace with its burning logs. If a guest should arrive, the servants without delay delved into large chests for cloth and hangings which they put in to make a partition. Nails were permanently embedded into the walls — many of them have been found — and contemporary accounts mention the number of hooks used when the king changed residence. It is more than likely that the tapestry hangers had a lot of work in the Val de Loire during the 15th and 16th centuries! Tapestries were an integral part of their baggage.

A wind from Italy

The great wind of change blew at the end of the 15th century when Charles brought back the riches of Italy with his army. By boatloads and cartloads, he brought back the immense plunder from his conquests beyond the mountains: 130 tapestries, 39 gold painted leather hangings, pieces of velvet and silk, illuminated books and sculptures. And that was not all: accompanying him and his suite came artists whose talent he admired: Domenico da Cortona (the famous Boccador), the sculptor Guido Mazzoni, the architect Fra Giocondo, the gardener Dom Pacello and included a parrot breeder, a cabinet-maker, an organ-builder, a tailor and even a manufacturer of artifical incubators!

Not that domestic architecture was deeply modified during these times; the greatest changes were in the field of decoration, with Italian features mingling with

The entrance hall of Langeais, with its high chimney piece and old beams is characteristic of the severe decoration of the 15th century. The tapestries portraying hunting scenes enliven the bareness of the walls.

old gothic foliated scrolls. Friezes, scallop shells, pilasters, fluted columns, antique arabesques, cornice stones, colonnades, loggias, galleries: a veritable orgy of decoration, perforated and chiselled stone and its crowning piece is Chambord, with its rare blend of Italian decor and a medieval structure. At the same time the art of gardening and the enchantment of water and forests were also discovered. Sometimes the French master craftsmen also adopted the more audacious elements of Italian architecture, like the balustraded staircases which replaced the spiral flights of stairs set in turreted towers. Naturally the king's taste became that of the court, and the great lords who could afford to do so, decorated their residences with pinnacles and large windows, friezes and mouldings...

Unfortunately festivities do not last, and more often than not these royal palaces were no more than an illustrious theatrical background which sprang into life on the occasion of a ball or hunt and then sank back into the mist on the departure of the court. The fires were put out, the tapestries rolled up, the ewers, flagons and silver plates piled up and the little procession disappeared at the end of the oak-lined drive. The court of the Valois already preferred Fontainebleau to the Val de Loire.

A marvel of elegance, the staircase in the Gaston d'Orléans wing at Blois rises beneath a sculptured ceiling ending in a rounded cupola. François Mansart adapted the straight staircase of the Italian Renaissance to classical taste.

The spiral staircase set in a projecting tower remained popular right up to the middle of the 16th century. Here, the monumental staircase at Saint Aignan, rolls round in a graceful curve within a polygonal tower.

Whiteness, moderation and symmetry characterize Cheverny : a Renaissance lay-out revised by classical taste. The disposition of stones in horizontal bands, the row of niches encasing statues relieve the somewhat heavy façade.

It really seems as if imagination flickered out after this burst of show. Creativity and art migrated towards the north along with the kings, and the Tourangeaux masons who remained were content to reproduce well-tried ideas. Of course the local tradition still inspired elegant dwellings but these were principally private residences, all the more atttractive for being small in size: Villesavin la Morinière, Poncé near Tours whose Renaissance staircase below a coffered ceiling attains a rare perfection; others served as country retreats for numerous gentlemen and their descendants. The Val de Loire was no longer at the heart of political decisions: political life belonged to the Ile-de-France. The king settled at the Louvre and art slowly forsook the grace and fantasy of the Renaissance to flow into the impressive mould of the monarchy of Louis XIV.

The great lords resided in Paris where they had their town houses and paid only short visits to the country; they chose the style created in the Ile-de-France for their mansions, straight lines, classical façades with pediments, paved courtyards and impeccable gardens traced as straight as a die. Menars and Cheverny are good examples of this style; they called on great Parisian artists such as Mansart, Soufflot and Gabriel. Furthermore, fortunes were often exhausted and many an old feudal dwelling, being difficult to adapt, provided shelter from financial ruin or for the miserable life of some gentleman in disgrace. The castles changed hands, and the French Revolution caused the destruction of more than one. But, in spite of these ups and downs, some families have managed to hold them on to their estates right up to the 20th century and spend all their money on the protection, restoration and upkeep of châteaux or *gentilhommières* which remain today, thanks to them, living residences.

The royal châteaux have had a much less enviable destiny: the Revolution did not always spare them and the Empire had no interest in them. Vandalism and groups of unscrupulous merchants made a meal out of them. In 1815, Blois was used as barracks, carts filled the courtyard; locks, metalwork and mantlepieces were stolen or salvaged to be used in the restoration of private homes. At Chambord the chapel was transformed into kennels; the unfurnished château was full of spiders and its pitiful condition caused Flaubert to write these sad lines: 'A feeling of grief takes hold of you at the sight of this misery bereft of beauty.' As for Amboise, it was partially destroyed at the beginning of the 19th century and as its restoration was considered too expensive, it was sold almost in spare parts: panes of glass, staircase steps, panelling, paving stones and bricks by lots of a thousand.

It was the archaeological societies of the 19th century and the cries of alarm from Viollet-le-Duc which alerted public opinion and the authorities. Restoration work was started with enthusiasm and sometimes to excess; there was a craze for medieval reconstructions which sometimes looked like iced wedding cakes. But this awakening of conscience bore its fruit: the wounds were attended to. In the 20th century the architects of historial monuments undertook their restoration using all their scientific knowledge. □

The transparent quality of the water gives the Loire countryside its special luminosity and reflects the red brick façade of the château de Gien between its grey pebbles.

Orléanais: the cradle of France

THE LOIRE CHANGES with each region and each traveller: sluggish or raging, grey or yellow, as clear as molten silver or hazy through the mist. Where shall we begin? Shall we accompany the pilgrim from Compostella and rest our tired feet in the nave of some abbey or the great hall of a castle, or follow the inspired footsteps of Joan of Arc? Or sit down to a plate of *andouillettes* with Rabelais before joining the fight against Picrochole, or accompany Balzac and Félix de Vandenesse as they go through the castles of Touraine, one by one, in search of Mme de Mortsauf?

From Gien to Ponts-de-Cé, the Loire takes liberties with history. She laughs at chronology and changes in style, progressing or slowing down at whim. And undoubtedly she is the best of the guides. She knows how to keep surprises in store for the visitor: moving from a Renaissance gem to an austere feudal power, from untamed violence to the delights of feasts. Those who follow her never tire: an accomplice to every whim, she adapts to changing scenery and tastes.

However, this is only once in a way: on entering the Orléanais, the Loire and history flow together. This is the cradle of France and the young Capetian monarchy: almost devoid of territory, surrounded by mighty barons, the king was above all a symbol of power and fragility. In the year one thousand, the domain of Hugues Capet consisted of the counties of Orléans and Étampes, the nucleus of his dynasty, and included a few small fiefs to the north. But the Capet family required the permission of its vassals to move about on its own estates! So they made Orléans their main residence and for two centuries, it remained

The Loire, a river 'of never ending waves of mottled water, of golden shores, supple lines, sometimes impetuous and raging like a wild animal and sometimes pretending to be sluggish...' (Ch. Péguy).

the capital of their kingdom. Along a green ribbon where the river snakes, solid fortresses were built, like sentinels on the look out for the enemy: Gien, Sully-sur-Loire, Châteauneuf, Jargeau, Meung and Beaugency. With their wooden or stone bridges, they are the gateways to the Loire, watchdogs of the kingdom and they still bear the scars of war.

Gien is where the Loire enters the châteaux country. She flows broad and majestic beneath the solid walls of the old square fortress. To the north, the alluvial plains of the Beauce spread their golden fields of corn as far as the eye can see, studded here and there with large red-tiled farms; this is where the Carolingians cultivated enormous tracts of land. Further to the east lies the forest, with its heathlands, ponds and deep valleys overgrown with ferns, a land abounding in game, with woods of oak and birch.

It is fitting to begin our discovery of the castles with Gien, the fortress of Anne de Beaujeu. In the Val de Loire the ladies are at home, whether they sit on the throne or discreetly share the king's couch in some hunting lodge. They set the tone. 'A court without ladies is like a garden without roses', said François I, a connoisseur on the subject. And, in fact, a large variety of roses were to bloom on the banks of the Loire!

Anne de Beaujeu was like a rose with thorns. Her only passion was politics. Brantôme describes her as authoritarian, deceitful and spiteful, like her father Louis XI, whose unvarnished praise was tempered by the misogyny of the age: 'She is the least foolish woman of France, as for wise ones, there are none.' Such qualities worked wonders when, in 1482, at the age of twenty-two, Anne assumed the regency in the name of her younger brother, thirteen year-old Charles VIII. A year later, *Madame la Grande,* as she was called, had to relinquish the royal seal, as fourteen was the age of majority. This is when she undertook the restoration of the old château of Gien, according to the fashion of the time with a decoration of red and black bricks. The work lasted more than five years, but Anne did not give up affairs, and with the help of her husband, Pierre de Beaujeu, she controlled the family property with a skill worthy of her father; then she made sure of the support of devoted vassals and retired to Moulins, where she encouraged the presence of artists. Louise de Savoie, a poor relation at her court, quietly bided her time or rather that of her son, François d'Angoulême. And while Charles VIII dreamed of chivalrous and Italian conquests, Anne de Beaujeu forged a solid network of alliances and built up her fortune. She did not abandon Gien in her days of prosperity: the town owes to her the reconstruction of the bridge, the château church, the Minim convent which houses an earthenware works, the convent of the Poor Clares, the chapel of Saint-Lazare. Unfortunately, the last war caused a lot of damage to the area situated between the château and the river.

*Henri IV
raised the ancient barony of Sully
into a duchy for his minister.
The great banker of the kingdom
lived the life of a prince
and wrote his memoirs there.*

Sully, a happy duke

A few kilometers away, let us jump a couple of centuries: here is the château of Sully. In 1961, a sign pinned on the door showed 'Château for sale'. After a close auction, Sully with its park and twelve outbuildings was sold for 654,210 new francs. The minister of Henry IV acquired it for 330,000 *livres*; no doubt that the greatest dignitaries of the kingdom knew how to increase their fortune! At his death in 1639, Sully, who always had a good head for figures, was to bequeath over five million *livres.*

When he bought the château, the minister to Henry IV was still Maximilien de Bethune, Marquis de Rosny. He owned a lot of land in the Orléanais, in the Beauce and Perche; he was governor of Jargeau and held the living of Saint-Benoît-sur-Loire where, as a devout Protestant, he had appointed a Catholic priest! In recognition of his services, the king desired to give him the title of duke. 'Sire', replied the minister, 'I would be a happy duke if, with the title you have just offered me, is attached the land I love the most, Sully.'

And so it was and the new duke displayed an inexhaustible energy in restoring his property: the roofs were tiled, paintings and wood-work adorned the rooms, gardens were laid out and ponds filled thanks to an ingenious machine which pumped water from the Sauge river, a small tributary of the Loire. The château with its solid towers and moat deserves its name which means 'stronghold'. The 14th century keep with

*Gracefulness and severity
of the château de Sully
set down like a watch-tower
at the gateway to Orléanais;
the river
which supplies the deep moats
provided an invulnerable defence.*

*The magnificent old roof-timbers
of the guardroom
of the château de Gien
shelter a hunting museum
and a collection of paintings
by François Desportes,
the artist of royal hunting scenes.*

its parapet walk and magnificent chestnut roof timbers still conjures up the Hundred Years War when La Trémoille was owner and tried to keep Joan of Arc within its walls. But, to the east, a small 17th-century château with two main buildings and a Renaissance style pavillion has retained a more attractive appearance.

Sully's amazing capacity for work is well-known. Rising at 4 o'clock, he spent the rest of the morning dictating notes to his secretaries; meals were served in the main hall according to the most formal etiquette: he and his wife occupied the place of honour in armchairs at either end of the table, while his guests were only allowed stools — at least this is what the spiteful Tallemant des Réaux affirms. The great

The 'young Arouet' had become Voltaire when Largillière painted him with his ironic expression and mocking smile. Voltaire produced his tragedy Artémise *in the great hall of the old château in 1719.*

In the 'old château' Georges de La Trémoille received Joan of Arc. He held her prisoner there some time, doubting her sincerity.

man had a few bad habits: haughty, vain and extremely proud of his illustrious lineage, he was detested for his pride. Tallemant once again describes his formal walks in the park before dinner accompanied by assidious courtiers: 'Fifteen old peacocks and seven or eight crafty old gentlemen at the sound of the bell get into a line of honour and then proceed to follow him...' One might almost be there!

From 1611 to 1617, during the long mornings of his retreat, Sully wrote his memoirs, the exact title being *Memoirs of wise and royal economies of State, domestic, political and military, of Henri the Great, an exemplary king, the prince of virtues, arms and laws and the true father of the French people.* He should not be accused of flattery! The minister was genuinely devoted to his king whom he served for over thirty years; but, nevertheless, he did not forget to justify himself—judicious charity! The first two volumes were printed in 1638 by printers from Angers who had installed their presses in the château. The cost of printing: 5,223 *livres,* a trifling sum in comparison with his acquired wealth and the judgement of posterity.

The château remained in the family for three centuries which is very unusual along the banks of the Loire (other examples are the châteaux of Luynes, Brissac and Cheverny). Among the illustrious visitors who came, the place of honour must go, in the 18th century, to a young man aged twenty-two, 'the young Arouet', who made too much fun of the regent and was advised, in 1716, to make himself scarce by retreating to the country. Two years later, the young Arouet was to become famous under the pseudonym of Voltaire. But, in the meantime, he swaggered in his retreat at Sully: 'There are perhaps some people who think that I am in exile, but the truth is that his lordship, the regent, ordered me to spend some months in this delightful countryside which attracts persons of merit in the autumn...' Boasting? He is more sincere when he writes: 'My stay here would be delightul if I were allowed to leave!' His confession recalls another one, just as sincere, made by Mme de Staël exiled some ninety years later at Chaumont whose beauty she also admired: 'Ah yes, but how much more do I prefer the gutter of the rue du Bac!'

Like the duc of Sully, but of lesser extraction—*noblesse de robe*—Louis II Phélypeaux, lord of La Vrillière, lord of Châteauneuf-sur-Loire, was an important servant of the state. The Orléanais overflowed with families who, in return for their services, received rich lands in the Beauce or the Sologne. The chancellor Séguier owned

A moss-covered bridge and a mass of foliage give a romantic air to the classical cupola of the château de Châteauneuf-sur-Loire, the only vestiges of the sumptuous residence of the Phélipeaux family.

Gien, and Châteauneuf, before it belonged to the Phélypeaux family, was owned by Particelli d'Emery, financial secretary to Louis XIII.

The wealth of the Phélypeaux family, natives of Blois, goes back to the 17th century: for two centuries, from father to son, they held either the post of state secretary, chief master of the ceremonies or controler of the Treasury. Louis II, one of the most ostentatious, had the medieval château of Châteauneuf rebuilt, where he collected furniture, tapestries and precious objects. Such prosperity due to the king's favour did not make only friends for the family, if we are to judge by this dry remark made by a neighbour about another Phélypeaux from Saint-Florentin in the 18th century: 'His devotion to the king and his sedentary tastes make him a nonentity, except for his position!'

In 1783, on the eve of the Revolution, the duke of Penthièvre, Admiral of France and well-known as a patron of the arts, bought Châteauneuf. But the events of 1789 sounded the death knell for festivities and balls. Weeds grew up in the park designed by Le Nôtre and the abandoned château was demolished in 1803. Today, all that remains of these hours of glory is a delightful domed rotonda, the forecourt pavilions and the magnificent displays of giant rhododendrons.

Meung-sur-Loire: a new art of loving

From Sully onwards, the Loire enters the marlstone area of the Orléanais, spreading out in wide curves which separate into a multitude of riverlets flowing between sandy banks before joining up again. Pasturelands, tiered vineyards and clumps of pines line the banks. In such a peaceful countryside sanctified by the marvellous abbey of Saint-Benoît, who would think of war? And yet, so many troops have passed through here, so many people fled across the centuries, most recently in 1944...

A place where the spirit moves, Saint-Benoît-sur-Loire was built during the 11th and 12th centuries, its Romanesque nave being completed in 1218. Tall columns, the span of broken arcades, the raised choir, the vault over intersecting ribs add to the harmony of the nave.

In 1429, the English and their allies, led by the Duke of Bedford, were on home ground in the Orléanais; they had reached Meung, Beaugency and Jargeau and could triumphantly sing the old song:

What is left for the sweet Dauphin?
Orléans, Beaugency,
Notre-Dame de Cléry
Vendôme, Vendôme

And yet, the morale of these victors before the open plain was low. A young peasant girl aged eighteen, a sort of a witch who fornicated with Satan and is dressed as a boy, has delivered Orléans on behalf of the young king Charles VII from under their very noses and by surprise. The English defeat was a piece of witchcraft. On May 8, the English soldiers began to withdraw, by May 11, they had to surrender Jargeau and by 15 they abandoned Beaugency. The retreat was complete. Small garrisons left behind broke up at the approach of the famous banner 'Jhesu Maria' and Suffolk was taken prisoner. Hereafter the way is open for Charles VII, and the 'sweet dauphin' received the sacred anointment at Reims which made him truly king of France.

Nowadays, these imposing towers high above peaceful blue and white villages have nothing sinister about them. Beaugency, one of the oldest, is a typical example of 11th-century military architecture and that of Meung is two centuries later. They are still filled with memories from the past associated with love rather than war.

The fortress of Beaugency, rebuilt in the 15th century, was the scene for the final chapter of a sad love story which turned into a political disaster. On March 18, 1452, the council at Beaugency annulled the marriage of Louis VII and Aliénor of Aquitaine. The marriage had, however, started under the most favourable circumstances: shortly after the young woman, one of the most endowed of France — the provinces of Aquitaine and Poitou were included in her dowry—accompanied her husband on his crusade to Palestine. But either too beautiful or too passionate, she could neither resist the voluptuous climate of the East nor the advances of an uncle prince of the country. Her husband was suspicious, cut short his stay and decided to divorce. In vain the Pope tried to save the situation: he made the king and queen sleep in the same bed, relates the author of *Historia pontificalis* and, nine months later, a

The square keep of Beaugency was built by Fulk Nerra. The postern gate on the first floor includes the storage rooms; on the second floor the lord resided; his followers lived on the upper floors and crenellations crown the building.

young princess was born. But, as Aliénor had not calmed down nor had Louis VII, divorce became inevitable. The council of Beaugency therefore annulled the union on grounds of consanguinity. In losing an unfaithful wife, Louis VII lost half of France; a vassal, Henry Plantagenet, was to get both.

The château at Meung belonged to the bishops of Orléans. The bishops did not take morals lightly and, in the château, all through the summer of 1461, chained by his feet and living off 'a small crust of bread and cold water', lay a thief who was also a poet, François Villon. Fortunately, Louis XI passing that way released him.

But there was another poet, quite respectable this time, a doctor in theology and yet no less subversive, who made the little town of Meung famous. His name was Jean Clopinel, better known under the name of Jean de Meung.

This fifty-year-old man took up the unfinished novel by Guillaume de Lorris around 1277, *Le Roman de la rose* and completed it with 18,000 lines. And what lines! Between much learned discussion, he slipped in sly satires about priests and monks and above all, in the name of Mother Nature, he made an all-out attack on courtly life and the cult of the inaccessible lady. Two centuries in advance of Humanism, his lover gathers roses while he may. His book was condemned by bishops and the old university doctor Gerson, but was to become one of the most widely read of all works until the 16th century.

Let us leave the Orléanais with this disrespectful parody of courtly ideals written by a critical bourgeois. It is only fair, because in the 15th century a whole world was in the process of breaking up, going bankrupt: that of the all-powerful knight, defeated at Crécy, Poitiers and Agincourt.

New horizons were appearing, leaving the field open to feminine influences: it is through women that genuine changes in customs were to take place in the 15th century. □

Le Roman de la Rose *was a best-seller in the Middle Ages. Jean de Meung gave the work a humanist conclusion : Love frees Bon Accueil and is captivated by Nature. The keep bears only a faint resemblance to the large square tower of Meung-sur-Loire!*

Blois: a museum castle

Beaugency is the real gateway to the valley of the Loire. The river widens and describes harmonious curves, flowing alongside gloomy woods and the marshlands of Sologne before spreading out between the vine-covered slopes and blooming parks: a country of transition where cultivated fields are few and far between and where the orchards of Touraine begin beneath an almost southern climate. A good country for eating, where Pantagruel would not have looked down on the traditional local specialities: wood-duck ragout, duck *à la solognote,* asparagus, carp from Chambord or salmon from the Val de Loire, all washed down with a delicious wine, the colour of rubies.

Gay, harmonious, full of fine people was how visitors in the past saw Blois, giving the lie to the famous saying 'Blois is a town of parvenus, gaily squandering their wealth'. The oldest lord of the place with the sad name of Thibaut the Deceiver, has passed from memory, people prefer to remember Charles d'Orléans, the poet prince to whom the town perhaps owes its tradition of refinement and sociability.

"... the river,
Widening its splendid basin below Blois,
Like a mother clasping her child to her breast
Quietly whispering with a meditative voice,
Encloses a delightful island in her enfolded arms" (Victor Hugo).

On the border of three regions, the Beauce, the Sologne and the Touraine, the château is also at the crossroads of many past ages; its architecture covers five centuries of history; a museum château, imitated by great lords anxious to bring their homes up to date. Some of the most tragic, fantastic and touching events of French history lie inscribed in its walls.

A poet and a thief

Blois was firstly the château of a poet, Charles d'Orléans. Purchased in the 14th century from the counts of Châtillon, the duke decided, in 1440, to make the old crenellated castle into a comfortable residence, a haven for artists and a peaceful retreat to rest his broken heart. Charles had had a very hard life, he was thirteen when his father, Louis d'Orléans, was assassinated by the hired men of John the Fearless; married at fifteen, he lost his young wife in 1409 and his second wife in 1415. To avenge his father's death, he managed to assemble troops by selling his family jewels and possessions, but he was wounded at the disaster of Agincourt and

Blois, a peaceful and agreeable town impregnated with the gentleness of the Loire. Everyone who visits Blois loves its white walls, the bricks and narrow streets, the gardens and numerous bell towers which ring out each hour in the mild air. Unfortunately the last war destroyed hundreds of houses.

taken prisoner by the English. Twenty-five years of captivity in the ice-cold dungeons of the Tower of London and in castles wreathed in mist, 'in black mourning is clothed my courage', he wrote in prison. He composed ballads to forget his suffering and finally managed to get together the ransom money required. Freed in 1440, he returned to France with all the sad joy one can imagine and settled at Blois. The work was completed in 1550 and in company of his new and very young wife, Maria of Clèves, he settled down.

The Loire is a soothing countryside. Charles led the life of a 'gentle lord' in his castle, he could be seen walking along the arcaded gallery, wearing a long fur-lined coat and composing poetry. If he was indifferent to protocol and loved above all greatness of heart and mind, he nonetheless took care to make his surroundings attractive. The knight's hall was covered with tapestries, and rugs from the East covered the floors.

One day, in the year 1457, a strange young man aged thirty presented himself to this refined society, 'dry and black like a snake', on his way back from Angers attracted by some doubtful business. His name was François Villon. A bad lot, a sort of rebel who haunted taverns and had a better knowledge of picking locks than of his teachers at the University where he had been a student. He is wanted for the murder of a priest with whom he had come to blows. But, already a year ago his *Lais,* had conquered the public with their bufoonery, clowning and poetic freshness. And between the old prince aged sixty-seven and the young thief on the run, a friendship grew up, nourished by similar tastes and beyond social differences.

Charles amused himself by suggesting themes for ballad contests to the charming company which surrounded him. His choice for François Villon seemed to inspire the poet: 'I die of thirst beside the fountain.' The lines written by the two contestants have been conserved, but it was Villon who won the prize. Fed, housed, pensioned, Villon is not the sort of man to wear a halter round his neck for long nor to sit motionless in front of a fountain! One morning, in May, he left without warning, and all trace of him was lost...

At nearly seventy, the duke of Orléans discovered at last the joy of having a son after two daughters. The child was named Louis after his royal uncle, Louis XI; the king himself came in person to hold the child at his christening. Nobody imagined at that time that the young Louis would one day be king, since the Dauphin, the future Charles VIII, brought up at Amboise, was in perfect health. Such an eventuality was so far from his mind that when his nephew was two years old, Louis XI decided to marry him to his own daughter Jeanne. Jeanne had a kind heart but she was mis-shapen and weakly and the marriage was more likely than not to remain without issue; in which case the possessions of the Orléans branch would revert to the French crown.

When the frail Jeanne, aged twelve, was presented to her future mother-in-law, Maria of Clèves, the latter almost fainted with horror. However the contract was signed on September 8, 1476, the archbishop of Orléans gave the royal couple his blessing in the château of Montrichard. The young bride later retired to Lignières where she had grown up and where her husband visited her twice a year, neither talking to nor looking at her. Poor Jeanne!

Blois becomes a royal residence

It is one of the quirks of history that the impetuous, wild Louis d'Orléans should have been married to this ugly humpbacked girl. The young man was considered one of the best wrestlers in the kingdom and he could jump five meters across the dikes of Châteauneuf-sur-Cher where his mother often stayed. Inconstant, frivolous, with an appetite for luxury and pleasure, how could he appreciate the inner qualities of Jeanne? Only ambition counted for this

This engraving shows the first edition of the works of François Villon in 1489 : poetry, disrespect, shrewdness. The author was not only a scholar who knew all about tradition, but also a sort of bohemian who defied the laws and customs of his age.

Courtly habits were maintained at Blois thanks to a refined prince, Charles d'Orléans, and to the court which his coquettish wife, Marie de Clèves gathered around her. Poetry and ballads were recited or sung in front of assemblies of gentle lords and young ladies wearing pointed hennins and long veils.

recalcitrant mind and he did not abstain from plotting: one might say he was impatient to wear the crown.

For once fate was kind. Just when he was about to be arrested for his intrigues, the king, Charles VIII, who was aged only twenty-eight, suddenly died at Amboise in 1498. His wife, Anne of Brittany, had not given him a son and Louis was his closest relation. What an incredible transformation; the scatter-brained trouble-maker that was the Duke of Orléans became Louis XII, a thrifty king, not to say mean, perhaps prematurely worn out by his youthful escapades. There was no question of sharing the throne with the crippled Jeanne, nor of letting the widow of Charles VIII, Anne of Brittany withdraw to her homeland taking the precious crown of Brittany with her. Pope Alexander VI solved the problem without being overscrupulous. He immediately sent off his natural son, Cesar Borgia with a magnificent retinue to Chinon—Blois was in full renovation—with the letters of annulment to the marriage of Louis XII.

With Jeanne divorced and retired to a convent, nothing stood in the way of Louis' marriage to the widow and her beautiful duchy. Anne of Brittany, matured by life,

In this delightful portrait painted on a wood panel, Anne of Brittany wears a Breton coif and a plain dress tied with a girdle. At twenty-three, she was the first queen to live at Blois.

On the left : *the moderation of the wing built by François Mansart contrasts strongly with the luxuriant fantasy of the François I wing. Gaston d'Orléans did not have the opportunity to stay there, residing in the back of the courtyard. Moreover, the building remained unfinished.*

In the centre : *sparkling white, entirely built of freestone, the François I wing contrasts with his predecessors' buildings; the staircase tower with open-work walls used to occupy the centre of the façade, but was displaced by the construction of the Gaston d'Orléans wing; its open-work balconies served as a tribune for the court on royal occasions.*

On the right : *the Louis XII wing, where the first traces of the Italian style may be seen, and, more restrained, the first floor gallery by Charles d'Orléans, harmonises with the warm brick decoration.*

was twenty-two when she became queen for the second time in 1499. As Blois lacked the comforts necessary to courtly life the king decided to reorganize the château completely by adding a wing; in the meantime the couple were to stay at Amboise. Louis, with praiseworthy attention to detail, ordered the director of the work, François de Pontbriant, to harmonize the new building with the wing already built by his father. Thus, the same combination of stone and brick, mouldings and arcades are to be found.

This same team of builders had already worked on Amboise, local men such as Colin Biart, Jacques Sourdeau, Pierre Trinqueau. The Italian influence can be seen in the decoration of pediments, dormer windows, the underlined cornice stones and arabesque panels, but the French masons retained the traditional technique of the Gothic flamboyant, cutting deeply into the sculptures which gives them the delicacy of pillow lace. As for the new gardens, arranged in terraces with a white marble fountain and the queen's small pavilion, they are a source of delight to Italian visitors.

The new château thus modernized became the favourite residence of the royal family. The apartments, modest in size, occupied the first floor. Tapestries, hangings, chests, silver and gold ware were brought from Amboise. The queen's room was hung with gold cloth and tapestries embroidered with strange animals. It adjoined the infant's room—that of the princess Claude born in 1499—whose walls were hung with a tapestry depicting a sheepfold. Beside the cradle, protected by a green damask canopy, stood the governess's camp bed.

The queen's household included some three hundred people, including some hundred ladies and maidens of honour belonging to noble and powerful families. Young pages, knights of Breton nobility, esquires, pantlers, cup-bearers, doctors, apothecaries belonged to her suite: the queen of France lived on a grand scale in her court. Very simply dressed in every day life — she wore a plain velvet dress tied with a nun's girdle, her hair covered by a small Breton pleated headdress — on official occasions, she donned magnificent costumes lined with ermine: the girdle and ermine were her emblems. As for Louis XII, social life did not seem to preoccupy him: wearing mid-length hair beneath a bonnet, and a short coat, his everyday costume was modest and his meals even more so: boiled beef!

The births, followed by the successive deaths of her children exhausted Anne who withdrew to the second floor in the buildings situated near the chapel, while her daughter Claude occupied apartments near her on the other side of a reception room. Claude's bedchamber was then hung with gold silk edged with the girdle and arms of Brittany; in the room were large carved chests, a high-backed wooden chair, a prayer stool, a Venetian mirror and on a dressing table, gold objects brought by her father from Italy. The royal family's tastes were simple.

Engaged at two years old

Anne of Brittany, beautiful and serious, also had a head for politics. Her main preoccupation, since the birth of the little Claude, was to find her a husband. A husband who would satisfy the requirements of rank, love and politics. What mother is not ambitious for her daughter? Now, the Archduke Philip of Austria and his wife Joan of Castille had just had a son, Charles, destined to rule

The Queen's apartment in the François I wing: the fleur de lys *decoration on the ceiling, the high chimney-piece with salamanders and ermine beneath a freize of scallop shells give an idea of the richness of the interior.*

Tournaments
were spectacles appreciated
by the court who admired
the skill of knights from the tribune.
Could the young Dauphin,
the future Henri II,
in honour of whom this tournament
was given,
have foreseen that he would perish
in a similar exercise,
twenty-five years later,
a victim to Montgomery's lance?

over an immense kingdom: Spain, Burgundy and perhaps the Empire. Although such a marriage project presented great dangers, Louis XII acquiesced with his wife's arguments; perhaps he gave way in the hope of having a son himself. In any case in 1501—Charles was one year old and Claude two—the future parents-in-law were entertained at Blois with all the solemnity due to the occasion: there was a line of archers, Swiss guards in glittering uniforms, trains of important dignitaries. Guards holding torches lined the way from the courtyard and up the staircase. Among the noble audience, a twelve year old child stood in the front row: François d'Angoulême, son of Louise de Savoie who, in the absence of a dauphin, was heir to the throne.

The Archduke jumped from his horse at the gate of the new main building, he was led into the great room on the first floor, decorated with tapestries and gold cloth where he made three low bows before the king. Louis XII embraced him. Then came the turn of the Archduchess to make her entry, she was led to the queen's apartments. A governess held the two-year-old fiancée in her arms followed by a procession of twenty young girls to present her to her future mother-in-law. The baby screamed—a bad omen? An escort of pages offered the ladies refreshments, sugared almonds and jam in golden jars. The meal was a light one as it was the vigil for Our Lady of Advent. Before bedtime tapestries were hung, a large green velvet chest was brought in containing all necessary toilet articles; mirrors, comb cases, sponge pots, Dutch towels and the beds were heated with silver warming pans.

The bad winter weather did not allow more than one hunt, but there were balls and tournaments. At last, on December 12, a Sunday, Louis XII and the Archduke Philip signed an agreement in the chapel of Saint-Calais. Claude was to be the wife of Charles, if God so willed. The agreement was renewed two years later at the Treaty of Blois.

However fate upset the plans. In the absence of a dauphin, opinion revolted against the idea that the Duchy of Brittany might pass through Claude's dowry, into the hands of the Habsburgs. French unity could not withstand such an eventuality. The Estates-General entreated Louis XII to break the agreement and offer his daughter to the heir to the throne, 'Monsieur François who is completely French'. In spite of protest from Anne of Brittany, the Austrian engagement was broken off in 1506, Claude was to marry François d'Angoulême in 1514.

No other queen or princess loved Blois as much as the gentle Claude of France; it was her childhood home and, in order to please her, her husband, the king, under took further improvements. François I required buildings sufficiently vast and sumptuous to house a continuously growing train of courtiers. Furthermore the new king, aged twenty, was as extravagant as his predecessor was modest. As an artist he loved all

What a cruel destiny for the gracious Claude de France! Abandoned by a roving husband, under the eye of her mother-in-law, Louise de Savoie, she went through seven successive pregnancies in ten years of married life and died at the age of twenty-five. Nonetheless, she was a careful administrator of her duchy of Brittany.

that was beautiful and, as a young man intoxicated by his fortune, he liked all that is new and brilliant. Blois owes to him, built on the former medieval building, the most original and detailed wing of the château which was added to the former medieval building, and whose magnificence rather overwhelms the simpler wing of Louis XII.

A marvel of inventiveness and delicacy

The octagonal tower, a marvellously delicate innovation, encloses a spiral staircase set into the façade like an open-work shell to break up the monotony. The building, under the direction of Raymond Phélypeaux, was entrusted to Jacques Sourdeau, master mason, who probably had advice from Domenico da Cortona concerning the decoration. If the architecture remains gothic, the horizontal lines which emphasize the floor levels, the sculptured pilasters of salamanders, the fluted columns and ornamental foliage are of Italian inspiration.

The façade was barely completed before it was clear that the accommodation was still insufficient and an additional building had to be constructed parallel, open on the outside and facing the north-west this time. Italian architects certainly participated, but their plans were clearly interpreted

The extraordinary rhythmic play of the horizontal and vertical lines of the façades of the loggias is best admired from the garden rails or from the terrace. At a distance, the lodgings give the impression of a Bramante style gallery, in fact, carved out of the thick wall, they do not communicate with each other. The campaign in Pavia put a stop to the building.

On first floor of the François I wing, the Cabinet des poisons named after 'Catherine de Medicis' with its 230 carved panels remained almost untouched. Four panels hide cupboards which were secret; they are opened by pushing a pedal hidden in the skirting-board.

the past, ɘ magnificent façade of the loggias minated the ravine and gardens, ɘ countryside lying just beyond, can be seen this 19th century engraving.

by French masons, which gives a unique stamp to the façade of the Loges. Overlooking moats and gardens, the two storey building, indented with alcoves and supported by slender pilasters surrounding the windows has the appearance of an Italian style gallery. At the top, a cclonnaded handrail supports the tiled roof and room is left for a promenade, the view from which extends far away to the city.

During his brief visits, the king occupied the second floor, the galleries along the inner courtyard were used for receptions and by the guards, while the private apartments look out onto the outer façade. Queen Claude occupied the first floor with her children; the Queen Mother Louise most probably lived in the Louis XII wing separated from the new wing by the State room. Claude barely had time to enjoy her palace because, on July 26, 1524, not quite twenty-five years old, she died, worn out by seven successive pregnancies.

After François I, the Valois did little to improve the château. Catherine de Medicis added a gallery on the ground floor of the new wing. She occupied part of the first floor overlooking the gardens and the town. Did she really use the famous cabinet called 'the cabinet of Catherine de Medicis'? In any case, the beautiful pannelled decor goes back to the time of François I; the walls are covered with two hundred and thirty wooden panels, delicately carved and in perfect condition, four of which open when a pedal hidden in the wainscoting is pressed: secret cupboards

Did Henri de Guise think that he would become king of France one day and succeed his cousin Henri III whose marriage remained sterile? More than likely. Energetic, with the physique of a hero in a novel, successful with women, he was the idol of the people.

where the queen is supposed to have kept poison, jewels, and state papers.

On the scene of the crime

Home of a poet and two grave and dignified queens, Blois was also the scene of a crime.

Let us imagine the terrible year of 1588. The Valois are going through the most serious crisis of their regime. The king, Henri III, is detested and despised, he is frightened by Paris which is unsettled, and by malcontents who plot against him. To safeguard his power, he sends six thousand troops into the city, with the Swiss guards, and has the city blockaded with iron chains. The people revolt and the Day of Barricades follows: the first signs of a far-reaching revolution. The frightened king leaves Paris, promising reforms, and convokes the Estates-General.

In fact, the real power is in the hands of the Duke de Guise, his cousin and childhood companion, who founded the Catholic League, to defend the Catholic faith and overcome the Reformation. A great leader, he unites under his banner all the malcontents of the kingdom. Cries of 'Long live Guise' fill the Paris streets. A family rivalry between cousins had turned into a terrible individual rivalry where the quarrel was not for the love of a woman but for a country.

In September 1588, the representatives of the three orders converge on Blois for the meeting of the Estates-General. The formal session starts after a three-day fast. The grand state hall, unaltered to this day, is hung with rich tapestries and violet velvet embossed with gold *fleurs de lys* covers the 13th-century pillars separating the hall into two equal parts. Beneath a portico, the lords and ladies of the court look on as spectators. There are more than five hundred representatives seated in order of precedence: 143 clergy, 180 nobility and 191 the Third Estate with a majority of League members. Everyone looks towards the tall Duke de Guise, dressed in white satin, as he advances bowing towards the wooden staircase which leads directly from the throne platform up to the royal apartments. He soon returns accompanied by the king and the royal princes. Henri III takes his seat on the throne, on his left sits his wife, Queen Louise, meek and unobtrusive and, on his right, the Queen Mother Catherine de Medicis, riddled with rheumatism and removed from power.

Right from the opening speech, Henry III goes on the attack by condemning the League and associations whose aim is to serve 'the unbounded ambitions of certain subjects'. The allusion is clear; the Duke receives the attack without a word, but he orders the phrase to be struck off the records. The atmosphere is highly charged and the sessions are noisy; the Third Estate complains of being burdened with taxes to provide for the insolent luxury of the court. The discussions get bogged down in December and even degenerate in this small closed world. Every day the Duke holds a semi-official council in his chambers where dignitaries keep him in touch with the latest news, and where he loudly prides himself on treating his royal cousin with insolence. Henri III submits to these disguised insults with rage in his heart.

Genuine fear can be felt in the overcharged atmosphere. Men of both sides sometimes even come to blows. In spite of an official reconciliation, disturbing rumours circulate which Guise brushes aside—he could not possibly dare to do it! On December 18 the Queen Mother, in spite of her illness, gives a magnificent banquet in honour of the engagement of her granddaughter, Christine of Lorraine. During the evening, Henri III disappears behind a curtain and climbs up to his study on the second floor by a secret staircase hidden in

The Salle des États *of the château de Blois has barely changed. In pure gothic style, it measures thirty metres long by eighteen metres wide; elegant columns with capitals divide it into two naves covered with wooden panels.*

the wall. Here he has his personal apartments just above those of his mother. In the François I wing, — the scene of the crime — the spatial arrangement has scarcely changed. The main staircase, on the right, leads to the guard room and the queen's apartments and, on the left, to the Council Chamber which was also used as a dining hall; the king's old study (demolished by Gaston d'Orléans) leads directly to the Council Chamber, but in November, the king had taken the precaution of walling up the door on his side, so no one could enter except through the royal chamber. Moreover, this room leads to all the others on the second floor. It is here that Henri often entertained his close friends and, it is here, on the evening of the banquet, that he rejoins several faithful followers who await him and urge him to act.

But he still hesitates. In public, he even gives signs of confidence in his cousin: he receives him in audience and reassures him of his intentions, swearing friendship after mass during which he took holy commu-

The chamber of Henri III was the scene of the crime: legend has it that the king hid behind the little door at the far end, close to the alcove used as an oratory. The room was greatly restored in the 19th century.

The staircase tower of the François I wing is octagonal in shape, three sides are linked to the construction. The interior is very richly decorated by columns with Corinthian capitals, and salamanders adorn the panels above each door leading onto the landing.

nion. And then he makes up his mind: 'The day after tomorrow is the day', he announces to the leader of the Forty-Five, his famous personal guard. It only remains to decide on the details of the plot. On December 22, the king gives out that he will leave the château at daybreak in preparation for the Christmas festivities and he begs Guise, Grandmaster of France, to give him the keys of the château. As he accompanies him to the door, he adds: 'Do not forget to come to the council early because we have many affairs to settle.'

The Duke of Guise is so unsuspecting that he passes the night with a beautiful lady and only returns to his apartments on the stroke of four in the morning. Although he hears unusual noises, he is not disturbed: no doubt the carriages are being prepared in the courtyard for the royal journey. December 23 dawns unpropitiously. Outside it is still dark, and a slight rain is falling. At about 6 o'clock, his secretary comes to draw the curtains and help Guise to dress. At 7, he climbs up the main staircase, stopping on the queen mother's floor to enquire after her health; he is led into the Council chamber where he is joined by several members of the royal guard. Not having eaten, he sends his secretary to fetch a box of Damascus grapes, while a valet rakes up the fire. At that moment Henry III sends for him to enter his old study.

The plot closes in on him. The Forty-Five are posted on the stairway, in rooms secretly prepared on the third floor and in the corridors. Eight armed guards wait in the royal chamber through which the Duke is obliged to pass. Guise has barely taken two steps when the eight men rush at him and thrust in their daggers. He struggles, calls for help and three minutes later collapses, murmuring as he dies: *Miserere Deus.* In the Council chamber, Guise's friends, alerted by the noise, attempt to rush to his aid, but the guards have closed all the exits and they force their prisoners up by a secret staircase to the next floor where they are to be massacred the following day. Meanwhile the king has returned to his chamber; he gazes at the blood-stained body lying on the floor and, touching it with the tip of his sword, makes his famous remark: 'My God, he looks even larger dead than alive!'

What an awful Christmas it was in

The reconstruction of the murder of the Duc de Guise by François Hogenberg is rather imaginative: one can see Henri III and his advisors in the old study, while Guise collapses at the foot of the royal bed.

1588! The assassination of Guise is made known in Paris on December 24 and from then on, open war is declared. Henri III has signed his death warrant. Astrologers see all kinds of disturbing signs in the sky. Ten days later Queen Catherine passes away, and on August 1, 1589, Henri III is assassinated by the avenging knife of Jacques Clément.

A fantastic escape

It is understandable that Marie de Medicis, a superstitious bigot, of limited intelligence, refused, in spite of its comfort, to install herself in the François I wing when her son Louis XIII, in 1618, asked her to withdraw from public affairs and remain at Blois. The bloody shadow of the great Guise still lingered in the royal apartments. So she decided to occupy the west side of the château (no longer surviving today and replaced by the Mansart building).

At Blois, Henri IV's widow brooded over the bitterness of exile. To be sure, she led the life of a queen with her personal seal and her officers, her Swiss guards in black uniforms and her court filled with constantly scheming Italians. Moreover, the château which had fallen into decay had been restored for her: glass destroyed by stormy weather replaced and an additional pavilion built of an intermediate style with study and dressing room. Nine heavily laden carts brought furniture and tapestries from her Louvre apartments.

One of the queen's favourite pastimes was taking care of her gardens at Blois, where she had orange trees planted, a green-house built and grew marvellous roses. Troops of comedians came to amuse her and musicians accompanied meals. Blois was a golden cage, but a cage after all. The queen stifled under the continuous surveillance ordered by her son. She was even forbidden to go into the town which was full of guards ordered to keep an eye on her coming and going; emissaries kept in touch with Paris and sent reports. Richelieu, who kept her company for some time, was requested to withdraw to his diocese of Luçon after certain manœuvres by Luynes. After some months, her situation as a prisoner seemed so unbearable to the impatient Marie de Medicis that when the priest Rucellai offered to organize her escape and put her under the protection of great and powerful men, she accepted.

This is the incredible escape, it reads like a cloak and dagger story. During the night of 21-22 February 1619, the comte de Brienne has hidden his carriage on the other side of the Blois bridge on the left bank opposite the château. At midnight, a few discreet taps on the window pane of the queen's bedchamber: M. du Plessis, secretary to the duc d'Épernon, announces that everything is ready for the escape, he is camped with a hundred and fifty mounted soldiers on horseback in a nearby village. A rope ladder is attached to the window and at 6 in the morning the queen, dressed as simply as possible, tightly clasping her jewel case to her breast, steps over the window balcony which looks out over the west terrace and starts to climb down. One can imagine this large bodied woman hampered by her skirts, swaying in mid-air at the end of a rope. More dead than alive, she reaches the terrace, quite determined for the last part of the climb—from the terrace to the foot of the château—to make use of another means of transport. Fortunately, at this point, dug out of the wall, there is a gentle slope due to recent works. Marie, with her jewel case, is tied up in a large coat and the packet is slid at the end of a rope to the bottom of the ditch. Her jewel case rolls down the slope, to be found by a servant the following morning. There is no question of stopping now. There is quite a long walk to reach the carriage on the banks of the Loire. Close to the river, in the early morning light, two or three peasants, early risers, watch this strange convoy go by and, mockingly, they joke, sure that it is a woman of easy virtue, they make a few lewd remarks; the queen bursts out laughing, but a few minutes later there is a panic: the carriage is not where it should be. In fact, the coachman has wisely hidden it a little further on. It only remains to get in and join Épernon at full gallop.

The king learns about the escape around 5 o'clock in the afternoon when he returns from hunting in the forest of Saint-Germain. Feelings run high. Meanwhile, the Queen Mother has reached Angoulême where the bishop of Luçon is to negotiate conditions for a reconciliation: Marie de Medicis demands freedom of movement, the government of Anjou and the citadels of Angers and Chinon, the guard of Ponts-de-Cé. After a few attempts at intimidation, Louis XIII finally agrees to see his mother in September 1619. The meeting takes place at Couzières in the château owned by the duke of Montbazon. The adventure has taught the incorrigible queen nothing, and she busily begins to intrigue once again.

The château of Blois lived its last hours of glory seven years later under the 'new master of the house', considered equally undesirable by the throne: Gaston d'Orléans. He was the younger brother of Louis XIII and has received Orléanais and Blésois in apanage, the revenues of which enabled him to live on a grand scale. When he was not plotting, he had a feeling for architecture and engineering; he erected a botanical garden, collected clocks and watches and his supreme ambition was to reconstruct the château completely from top to bottom. Mansart was sent for and suggested plans: part of the Charles d'Orléans west wing was demolished in 1635-1638 at the cost of one and a half million gold francs to make room for the building we can see today. Future generations have been highly critical of the Mansart pavilion and many are relieved that economies enforced by Richelieu stopped Gaston from completing his original project. It is at Blois that Gaston d'Orléans, permanently in disgrace, spent the rest of his days. Peaceful days at last, divided between hunting, the friendship of scholars, the cultivation of rare plants (tomatoes and tobacco) and boat excursions on the Loire. He died in 1660 from an apoplectic fit. □

Gaston d'Orléans lacked neither charm nor attraction; but posterity was to be severe, even unjust about the wing he had had built by François Mansart: 'classique de collège', *cried Flaubert, who added: 'his restrained taste is poor taste'.*

Chambord: for such is our

A WHIM? A STROKE OF MADNESS? What strange fantasy drove François I to build a château as large as a town in the heart of a dense forest, full of shrubs, thorn bushes, heathlands and marshes? The Cosson river was no more than a small reed-filled river full of croaking frogs and the old towers of the fortress of Thibaut the Deceiver were cracked and falling into ruin. Nothing could be more solitary or melancholy than these wooded wastelands.

And yet, it was here, in 1519, that the extravagant king decided to erect the fairy-tale château of Chambord whose golden gables are silhouetted against the sky at the end of the drive between the gold of the oaks and the copper beeches: 'for such is our pleasure'.

One is overwhelmed by the tremendous size of the enterprise and its unnecessary luxury. The king rarely stayed there more than three days at a time: in 1529, in 1530—he stayed almost a whole month with his new queen Eleanor—a few days in 1534 and, then in 1539 for the great demonstration of power before Charles V. The château was still not finished and moreover it was to be abandoned before the construction was complete. As for comfort, an obviously relative notion, it was been sacrificed to magnificence: 440 rooms, 83 staircases, of which 13 are main ones, 365 windows, galleries open to draughts, the entire building could neither be heated nor furnished. While the Blois apartments retained reasonable proportions, Chambord can only be seen as a sumptuous background for festivities.

A miracle of art and craftsmanship

The project naturally required considerable means: it took twelve years, 20,000 workmen and hundreds of thousands of *livres* to

pleasure

The mirage of Chambord: beneath its rows of windows chiselled like jewels, it seems to rise like an echo from the depths of the forest where ivory trumpets sound the death call.

bring to completion; this 'colossal folly', as Viollet-le-Duc called it. At one point, the king thought of diverting the Loire (four kilometres away) to make it flow in front of Chambord. He gave up the idea and decided to canalize the small river Cosson; its diversion feeds the moat and ponds. Its banks were enlarged at the bottom of the staircase so the court could make boat excursions. The marshland also had to be drained as the river seeped into the fields; the château is built on piles so there are neither cellars nor underground passages. Then the forest was torn apart to make long avenues, rides were cut out and, for the first time, this immense estate of 5,000 hectares was enclosed with high walls: thirty kilometres long, with six gates from which led six avenues.

His contemporaries themselves made no mistake: nothing like it had been seen anywhere before. 'A background for the fairies Morgane and Alcine', wrote the Venetian ambassador in 1577. 'The entire human industry of its age' as Charles V would have said. And Rabelais used it as a model for his description of the abbey of Thélème although the 'said building was a hundred times more magnificent, because it contained 8,332 rooms'. In short, as Brantôme said, Chambord is one of the 'wonders of the world'.

Who drew up the plans? It is a controversial question, but the greatest names have been suggested. Perhaps the ageing Leonardo da Vinci, a few months before his death, came as a neighbour from Amboise to examine the place. He was a friend of the king and had already done work at Gaillon for the cardinal of Amboise, he had taken part in drawing up plans for the château of Romorantin. As for Domenico da Cortona, called the Boccador, he was the author of a wooden scale model which we know of through a drawing by Félibien in the 17th century. These two Italians often worked together which would explain, according to some historians, the absence of an overall plan by Leonardo himself. The name of Primaticcio has also been suggested. One thing is certain, that the castle is based on a plan resembling that of St. Peter's at Rome: two naves crossing one another at right angles and set in the space between the arms are the royal apartments.

The master masons are known to us and they were definitely French: Sourdeau father and son, Pierre Neveu called 'Trinqueau' and Jean Gobereau; François de Pontbriand, governor of Blois and Loches and Jean Le Breton superintended the building work. They were to achieve an admirable

The rooftops of Chambord resemble a miniature town. The thirty-two metre lantern which crowns the central staircase, emerges amidst a forest of gables, dormer windows, chimney stacks and little bell towers. The court used to enjoy climbing up to the terrace in order to admire the forest expanse and to follow the start of a hunting party.

'he sculptor's chisel
as undercut the stone
'ith a virtuosity full of fantasy,
utting out niches or shells,
aventing innumerable floral motifs,
ittle spotted eagles and salamanders,
'hile the slate inlaid work
leams like a mosaic in the sunlight.

The northwest tower and the gallery linking it to the keep were begun under the reign of François I, but finished by Henri II who completed the building with a supporting wing and a corner staircase symetrical to the one in the northeast wing. The dome remained unfinished; caryatids were to have represented the king, Diane de Poitiers and Catherine de Medicis.

union between the French and Italian genius. It has often been said that Chambord is a unique combination of a Gothic castle as its base with the Italian decorative style in its terraces.

The overall layout still resembles a fortress, similar to those habitually built along the banks of the Loire. The square-shaped castle built of soft Bourré stone is confined by four towers and flanked by a surrounding wall which also has four corner towers. In the centre of the castle rises a double spiral staircase, each stairway twined round the other but independent, so that people can go up and down without meeting. This technical masterpiece was inspired by Leonardo, who has left us a sketch showing that he had at first designed a staircase with four spirals. This initial project was abandoned because it was clear that if the wrong staircase was taken one would have to go all the way down to the ground floor. The staircase leads to the terraces topped by a central thirty-two metre high lantern, crowned by a two meter *fleur de lys*.

The king added side buildings to the castle, linked by symmetrical galleries to the east which formed his royal apartments—only completed three years before

his death—the large chapel in the north-west tower was to be completed by his son Henri II. The latter gave Chambord its final important building, more austere and classical, the Henri II wing, with access by a spiral staircase identical to the one in the François I wing, with two stories of loggias. After him little work was done at Chambord.

'Women are fickle'

Chambord, a hunting lodge, awakens amidst the mist of a fine December morning to the sound of horns and a flourish of trumpets. François I arrives with his train of great lords, crowds of courtiers and ambassadors. From a long line of carts, valets unload piles of victuals: fruits arranged in pyramids, oysters, fish, wildfowl and casks of wine. Other servants set up

Beneath the cradle vault decorated with F's and salamanders, the twin spirals of the double staircase rise simultaneously without ever meeting, but one can catch a glimpse from the central column and the open-work balustrade. Originally, the staircase which went straight up the terrace was isolated, but for security reasons planks joined it each floor.

Dressed for a parade, a sceptre in his hand, this was how the court saw François I on horseback in front of his château. His ostentation made people forget his political mistakes, and his receptions at Chambord were part of his diplomatic policy.

trestle tables and still others unload chests and hang precious tapestries woven with gold thread over the walls; perfume is burnt and enormous tree trunks burn in the fireplace spreading a red glow over the panelled ceilings.

It takes no great feat of imagination to picture, caught in a shaft of light, outriders and horsemen cantering through the beech trees in pursuit of game. The old deer leaps over ferns, the king gallops, escorted by his 'little band' of men, in breathless pursuit and dangerous chase amongst the brushwood, which scratches and tears. The dogs bark when they catch scent of the trail; far away, the sun illuminates with a pale golden light the mass of turrets, dormer windows, chimney stacks and pinacles on the roofs of Chambord, like another forest made of stone, slate and copper. But the lords, intent on following the scent of their game, only have eyes for the gorse trampled underfoot by the horses' hooves in their chase. In spite of the beauty of the palace and the richness of apparel, in spite of lutes and serenades, they are still brutal-mannered men, intoxicated with air and war who wear themselves out for the ultimate reward: the deer at bay and the disemboweled boar.

Today Chambord is still one of the most important game sanctuaries in France with 700 deer and 990 boars; but people mostly hunt with a camera. Observation posts have been set up to facilitate the observation of animals, and if you walk out at dawn or dusk along the paths, you may surprise a cautious doe or fallow deer browsing amid young shoots or in the pasture land in search of food.

It is from the east wing and the north-east tower that we may catch a glimpse of François I's every-day life when he stayed at Chambord. His chamber, of majestic proportions, has an extensive view over the river through wide windows. A gently rising staircase decorated with salamanders leads to his room — the salamander motif is to be found by the hundred all over Chambord, an insistent witness to the greatness of François I. Attached to the royal chamber is a dressing room, a washroom and toilet. Dark corridors link the wing to the rest of the castle while a hidden staircase gives access right down to the château moat. Could it be a secret passage to protect the king's amorous intrigues, or some mysterious rendez-vous? Feminine associations are not absent from the gallant knightly king. To which lady did he refer, the brown-haired majestic Françoise de Châteaubriand or the gracious Anne de Pisseleu, Duchess d'Étampes, when he carved these disillusioned lines, noticed by Brantôme, on the window: 'women are fickle' ? The lady of Châteaubriand had already been replaced in the royal heart when Chambord was built and the king sent her away with these scarcely amiable lines:

For the time I spent with you
I can say, rest in peace

On the other hand, the fair haired Anne de Pisseleu had in her favour the freshness of youth, eyes like forget-me-not and considerable tact which helped to serve the political intentions of the king. Was she not seen talking familiarly with Charles V when he crossed France on his way to Flanders?

In December 1539 the Loire valley and particularly Chambord, of which only the central castle is complete, are exceptionally animated to receive Charles V. What a welcome! What pomp surrounds the procession! The most brilliant and amusing members of the court are present: Queen Eleanor, the second wife of François I, the Queen of Navarre, the Dauphin Henri and his wife Catherine de Médicis, Jeanne d'Al-

One cannot visit Chambord without recalling the bands of horsemen riding behind the king or throwing down roe-buck or doe at the feet of the ladies on the esplanade. Here everything reminds one of hunting, the tapestries, the trophies...

bret, the Duchess d'Étampes, a crowd of princes and princesses. The High Constable of Montmorency has been ordered to prepare Chambord, and, for three days, hunting parties and festivities follow one another. Then on December 19, the royal suite makes its way to Notre-Dame de Cléry on pilgrimage. Tents and tapestries are loaded on to carts, the fires extinguished and Chambord left to its mists.

François was to stay there again in 1541, 1543 and 1545: by which date his own apartments were just about finished. But already he had a new passion — Fontainebleau — and was devoting all his energy to its alteration.

Turkish scenes at Chambord: *Le Bourgeois gentilhomme*

History remembers Chambord for these short-lived festivities, brilliant like fireworks, but in between times, abandon and dilapidation were the everyday reality. In the 17th century water seeped through the terraces and rotted the ceilings, the walls crumbled away. An inventory made in 1685 indicates the scarcity of furniture: one red velvet armchair, thirty chairs, some folding chairs, one red velvet couch, eighteen stools, eight mirrors, six basins, four chamber pots, forty chandeliers, eighteen of which were broken, thirteen tables... it's not much for four hundred rooms!

However the château livened up again when Louis XIV stopped by in 1660 on his return from Saint-Jean-de-Luz. Without doubt the residence pleased the kings because of its links with the Valois festivities and its grandeur, and when it was reattached to the crown on the death of Gaston d'Orléans, the king decided to set about the urgent repair of the terraces and arranging the royal apartments on the first floor of the castle, the upper floor being reserved for important dignitaries.

Eight years later, Chambord shone once again for splendid festivities forgotten for over a century; the royal couple stayed there with their court for two weeks during September. 'There were comedies, balls and great suppers, never had the court been so entertained'. Of course, hunting was the king's favourite pastime; and his retinue dressed in blue lined with red and gold and silver braid, were lined up in the forecourt. The king enjoyed hunting deer as much as shooting partridges, and he was an excellent hunter, always eager for a chase in the open air. The mornings were

The ravishing Anne de Pisseleu was lady-in-waiting to Louise de Savoie. François I fell in love with her on his return from captivity in Spain; he made her Duchesse d'Étampes in 1536. She was called 'the most beautiful of the educated ladies and the most educated of the beautiful ladies'.

At Chambord, Louis XIV was to discover the same pleasures as François I: open-air life, big hunting parties, receptions in the evening. The château is sufficiently vast to house hundreds of cavaliers and their suite. It was also at Chambord that Louis XIV signed, in 1685, several ordinances against the Huguenots.

spent in long rides; they usually returned to dine at midday, but the king dined alone. In the evening, torches and chandeliers lit up the galleries of the château and parlour games provided entertainment. Then supper to music, before joining in a ball or watching a comedy. During the royal visits a theatre was constructed in the guard room on the third floor and the king's box was installed on the stairway hung with tapestries.

Molière accompanied the suite during these visits to Chambord. He was still the king's favourite, but controversial discussions concerning *Tartuffe* as well as pleurisy had undermined his health, so he only produced light, rapidly composed comedies which nevertheless bear the hallmark of his genius. Was *Monsieur de Pourceaugnac* played for the first time at Chambord on September 6 1669, written in one month during Molière's stay? Nobody knows, but in any case this *divertissement* combined with ballets composed by Lully was highly appreciated: grand ladies and handsome lords took great delight in this farce, which was a little coarse with its references to enemas as well as in Lully's fooling about when he jumped from the stage onto his harpsichord, completely wrecking it.

The following year, Turkish scenes were favoured by the public, *Le Bourgeois gentilhomme:* an icy silence greeted the first performance, all the courtiers turned towards the king to see if he was laughing, but the king remained expressionless, thoughtful or perhaps taken aback. However, he asked for a second performance and the play was performed three times in eight days, and was a great success.

The Dauphin's illness hastened the departure from Chambord and the king and his court left on October 22. Twelve years passed by before Louis XIV returned there again: war and the construction of Versailles having kept him occupied elsewhere. But he did not forget Chambord and, in 1682, he was back again, completely satisfied with the alterations to the château. In fact Mansart had raised the outer wall of the castle in order to build small lodgings, the famous 'mansardes', attics intended to house servants and officers. Although useful, the addition did not really enhance the château and were later demolished. Several projects were put forward, but the financial situation hindered their realization. Moreover, a festering boil forced the king to give up his grand hunting parties.

Chambord remained empty during the first twenty years of the 18th century. In 1725, Louis XV offered the château to his parents-in-law, Stanislas Leszczyński and his wife Catherine, dethroned from Poland and in exile. This little provincial court was, no doubt, a poor compensation for the royal couple. And yet Stanislas went through a lot of trouble to renovate the château and its park. He gave feasts and a ball for Shrove Tuesday. In the days following the reception, several guests fell ill with a heavy head and attacks of a strange fever. Was the dancing responsible? At the beginning of spring, the wind brought disagreeable fumes from the nearby marshes and moats which during the hot summer months, turned into stinking vapours. Stanislas himself suffered from rheumatism and more than fifty servants fell ill. The Leszczyński couple were obliged to leave this unhealthy spot. The bishop of Blois offered them the hospitality of the episcopal residence and they found refuge in the château of Menars. They only returned to Chambord in the autumn, and Stanislas Leszczyński attempted to improve the place by filling in the ditches, the source of the putrid fumes; but every summer, the Polish sovereigns moved away to the opposite side of the Loire.

Life is a dream

Although no king, Maurice de Saxe, the new master of Chambord, acted like one. And although the inhabitants have seen a lot, they can scarcely believe their eyes! In the château forecourt, thousands of soldiers, of all colours, from Europe, Asia, Africa; Turks and Uhlans and dragoons parade to the sound of a fanfare played by Martiniquese and Senegalese drummers. These are the 'Saxe volunteers', the personal regiment of the Maréchal, they have accompanied the victor of Fontenoy to his new residence. The inhabitants of Blois were to grow accustomed to this spectacle, so much so that in the following years the population included a few more babies, with brown skin and almond eyes.

In recompense for his brave military actions, Maréchal de Saxe received the exceptional privilege of being allowed to keep his regiment. Louis XV had Chambord magnificently restored and gave him

The Maréchal de Saxe, painted by La Tour, was a legendary lover. He lived the life of a prince at Chambord, entertaining his beautiful lady friends, the famous Mme Favart, Mlle de Sens, Mlle de Verrières, the Princesse de Conti... He was to offer them hunting parties, balls and comedies.

an allowance of 40,000 *livres,* which added to the income of the estate, enabled the Maréchal to live in grand style.

Nothing was too good for the natural son of Auguste II who joined the French, a kind of Hercules, as skilled in gallantry as in arms. His personal service included thirty-five officers and, like a sovereign, he dined alone before a magnificently laid table in front of his court and curious onlookers; after his dinner, tables were set up and the guests invited in. The Maréchal organized a magnificent hall for the theatre with 1,800 seats, its decoration cost 600,000 *livres.* His box was situated in the middle of the stage, far more sumptuous than that of Louis XIV. The daily routine included hunting and exercices on horseback; every day the trumpet rang out to announce manoeuvres beneath the Maréchal's banner. The stables numbered four hundred horses and around two hundred mares; horse-breaking parties were organized in the middle of the forest for wild horses. A princely style of living.

Were women responsible for the downfall of the handsome Maréchal? In November 1750, he suffered from an inflammation of the lungs due to the damp forest mists. His doctor, Sénac, was summoned urgently; he let out blood, but his patient's condition worsened and on December 2, Maurice de Saxe died, pronouncing these words, which so aptly apply to Chambord: 'Life is only a dream... Mine was good, but short'. Six cannons firing every fifteen minutes announced the sad news. The Marquis d'Argenson wrote in his diary: 'Yesterday we heard about the Maréchal de Saxe's death. After having blood let, he became swollen and died all of a sudden on Monday evening.'

A simple congestion of the lungs? Why did Grimm, who was staying at the château, give a different version of the facts? This is what he related: the Maréchal, really in poor health, received a letter one evening, he immediately got up and left, accompanied by his aide de camp, by a secret staircase. In a corner of the park two strangers awaited him in front of a post-chaise. They briefly exchanged greetings, Saxe drew his sword as did one of the strangers, the other stranger and his aide de camp acted as witnesses. A few minutes later, on his return to the château, the Maréchal came across his nephew; deathly pale and wounded, he mumbled a few words: 'Is the Prince de Conti still here? Please assure him that I have nothing against him. I request the utmost secrecy concerning what has just happened.' The sick man was taken to his room and three days later he died. Is Grimm's version of the story true to fact? Was the over-seductive Maréchal de Saxe victim to a jealous husband? His relationship with the princess of Conti was common knowledge. But the doctor's version does not necessarily contradict Grimm's one: wounded in a duel in the forest of Chambord, the Maréchal de Saxe, worn out by a dissolute life and vulnerable, was carried off by a congestion of the lungs.

The Maréchal was one of the last famous hosts of Chambord. The château was in the hands of the Polignac family when the Revolution broke out. A symbol of the detested monarchy, its furniture was ransacked in 1793; the floorboards, mantelpieces, and few remaining pieces of furniture were destroyed. A commission under the Directory suggested hammering out the *fleur de lys* in the château. Fortunately, the cost of such an undertaking caused them to give up the idea, but as it would require a considerable sum to repair the damage, things were left as they were. Maréchal Berthier, who had a right to the château, did not stay there and under the Empire, the buildings served merely as coach houses.

In 1821, a subscription allocated this enormous tumbling-down residence to the Duke of Bordeaux who spent all his money on repairing the ruins. The château once again became the focal point for royal hope: the crown was offered to the Duke of Bordeaux who had become count of Chambord. In the autumn of 1873 carriages

awaited in the courtyard, ready to carry the new king to his destiny. But, all merely the colour of a flag, France was to remain a republic: Henri V refused to relinquish the white flag of Henri IV.

Poor Chambord! It was offered to everybody, Stanislas Leszczyński, Maréchal de Saxe, Polignac, Berthier, Duke of Bordeaux, as if no one wanted it. 'It hardly seems to have been occupied', concluded Flaubert, 'like an abandoned inn'... The State however did want Chambord and in 1930 bought it up for eleven million francs and undertook its restoration. □

A stone gem set in a green jewel case. The plan of the château can be clearly seen from the air. The winding Cosson river has been transformed into a rectilinear canal, but the moats were filled in by Leszczyński. The two corner towers of the southern wing were kept low to open a vista.

Chambord, shining white like a fairy castle, has inspired Romantic poets. Châteaubriand compared it to 'a woman with her hair blown loose by the wind', and Vigny, to 'a magic château' stolen by an oriental genie.

servants richly rewarded

It is a common place to say that power and closeness to power breed wealth. The will of Florimond Robertet, a friend and servant to François I, is an eloquent testimony: on page after page are listed jewellery, furniture, tapestries accumulated in the château of Bury while in office and which he bequeathed to his wife. For this reason, the great servants of state have, through the ages, always attempted to settle near royal homes.

Over three to four decades the Val de Loire became covered with châteaux, the families of Robertet, Briçonnet, Bohier, Berthelot, Semblançay and many others, intoxicated by their success, had superb residences built, less than an hour's ride from the Valois palaces. Although Robertet was sufficiently wise to reflect on his motto: 'Remember the fate of ordinary men', others, because they did not, were less fortunate. And so Jacques de Beaune, baron de Semblançay, ended his days on the gallows at Montfaucon with a rope around his neck. His cousin, Gilles Berthelot, Lord of Azay-le-Rideau, narrowly escaped the same fate.

Those who avoided these difficulties invite us to visit their residences. Jean Le Breton was President of the Council of Accounts of Blois, a local man of standing, promoted secretary to the king. François I appointed him overseer of the construction of Chambord and made him responsible for the finances. As work on Chambord

At Villesavin, the Renaissance style already prefigures classicism with its harmonious proportions. But the gracious carvings of the dormer windows and the spiral staircase recall the influence of Chambord. The lead roofing was replaced with slate by Napoleon.

'he pool is the heart of Sologne. A light mist floats above the water where brushwood is reflected: an immobile, mysterious countryside animated for an instant by the flight of a wood-cock or partridge rising out of the damp woods.

went on for years, Le Breton, who already owned the beautiful château of Villandry, erected a more modest residence, close to the building site, which nonetheless shows the influence of its grandiose neighbour in certain details. A typical example of the Loire school, the work was started in 1537 by Florentine and French workers from the royal castles.

Long and low, firmly set in the Sologne soil, the residence of Villesavin is surrounded by green fields, clumps of box and pinetrees, the heaths and pools of Sologne. It exudes the mysterious atmosphere of *le Grand Meaulnes.* A basin made of Carrara marble adds a bright touch to the inner courtyard. In February 1541, after having spent a few days at Chambord, François I asked to be lodged by his secretary who received him at Villesavin; the king thoroughly enjoyed staying in the homes of his faithful friends, whose gracious dwellings made a change from monumental palaces. He also stayed in the fortified house of Herbault, and later at the home of his faithful Babou, la Bourdaisière. He even granted Babou 1,800 *livres* to enable him to add a second square pavilion in order to receive the king. It is true that the attractive Marie Babou was a more than likely reason for his choice.

Villesavin, with its high roofs cut up by pedimented gable windows, is a welcoming residence. On the left rises a dovecote set on a pedestal with 1,500 pigeon holes, called *boulins.* It used to be a noble

A vertiginous structure, the home of pigeons. The dove-cote is a noble privilege, and a few well-preserved examples are still to be found, like this one at Poncé or the one at Villesavin.

privilege to possess a dovecote and the wealth of the owner was measured by the number of pigeon holes. As their number was strictly proportional to the area of the estate, it can be estimated that the master of Villesavin owned approximately 950 hectares, which was common at this time. Rearing pigeons brought in a good income from the pigeon droppings in an age when chemical fertilizers were unheard-of. Roasted, stuffed, or as pâté, pigeons make an excellent dish, which they certainly knew how to prepare at Villesavin if we are to judge by the kitchens, where an ingenious Dutch invention which turned the spit can still be seen.

Beauregard, six kilometers from Blois, is the home of a powerful parliamentary family. They owed their rise and fortune to Jean de Thiers, State secretary to Henri II, a man of great taste and culture, according to

On a slope in the valley of the Beuvron, on the outskirts of Sologne, Beauregard was first of all a hunting lodge. The alterations made by different owners have turned it into this impressive construction, almost classical, which seems to come alive beneath the glinting sun.

The Grande Mademoiselle, *passing through Beauregard, wanted, it was said, to figure in this portrait gallery, but Louis XIV refused. Jean Mosnier, from Blois, painted the panelling work beneath the portraits. Delft tiles depicting Louis XIV's army, complete this magnificent decor.*

exquisite but unpretentious building, who could think of war? Terrassed walls, loopholes, crenellations, battlements, machicolations are merely ornamental and the walls are less than a metre thick. Ponds supplied the moats and provided a reservoir of water for the mill; they were drained in the time of Louis XIII.

The love affairs of poets

René des Roches was far from being as important or official a person as the prece-

Built on a terrace surrounded by a brick wall, the little château du Moulin at Lassay, consisting of two separate wings seems to rise out of the water; the main building is four stories high, while the gatehouse with a corner tower and drawbridge leads directly down to the moat.

Ronsard, who praised his refinement. Jean de Thiers turned this ancient hunting lodge into an agreable residence with a double gallery decorated with pilasters. The interior decoration is as delicate as that of the exterior; a carpenter from Fontainebleau — an indication of the notable connections of the lord of the château — drew up the design for the remarkable oak panelling in the Bell Study: below a panelled ceiling bearing the family arms, panels of wainscoting decorated with leather and lined with gold are adorned with little bells. The chapel, unfortunately destroyed in the 19th century, was covered with frescoes. In 1617, the State counsellor Ardier undertook new additions; he had the present-day façade built overlooking the Beuvron river, and he commissioned the decoration of the first floor from an artist who painted, according to the fashion of the day, a remarkable gallery of historical portraits, 365 celebrities from Philippe de Valois to Louis XIV, are arranged in three rows.

A few kilometers from Beauregard, off the tourist track, lies the little château du Moulin. It is impossible not to fall in love with it straight away. It had its moment of glory a long time ago, at the end of the 15th century, when its owner, Philippe du Moulin, rescued king Charles VIII at the battle of Fornovo di Taro. He also rendered many services to Louis XII and was allowed to fortify his residence in 1490. Jacques de Persigny, a mason from the court, drew up the plans, using all the latest architectural innovations of his age. Surrounded by moats and a terrassed wall, flanked with corner towers, the château has two perpendicular wings decorated with lozenge-shaped bricks alternating with lines of micaceous chalk stone. In front of this

The shadows of Cassandre and Ronsard hover round Talcy. The gallery was influenced by the Charles d'Orléans gallery at Blois. The well, surmounted by a dome lends a gracious note to the inner courtyard.

ding castle owners. This gentleman from Blésois was obliged to call on local masons of the region to erect the château de la Morinière, in which several features have been borrowed — not without some clumsiness in their imitation and execution — from Villesavin, the château du Moulin and even from Chambord. It was the fashion then, when unable to build an entirely new château, to add some 'Renaissance' detail, in the form of a freize, pediment or small gable to one's old residence. At the end of a long drive shaded by a vault of trees, rises an asymmetrical square building surrounded by moats. The château was built on two sides; the low wing dates back to the 15th century and is attached to a corner pavilion running parallel to a separate building. At the back of the courtyard the main building has only one floor surmounted with a slate roof and embellished with a decor of pediments and stone gables. The lantern at the top of the staircase is a rather poor imitation of that at Chambord and, the alternating pattern of bricks and chalk stone is reminiscent of Herbault or Moulin. The building was completed in 1548, the date is inscribed on a lock on the main building gate.

In 1548, Pierre de Ronsard was twenty-four, he was nephew by marriage to René des Roches. So la Morinière was not entirely unfamiliar to him and there is no doubt that he appreciated the intimate charm of this country mansion with its outbuildings built of pink bricks covered with mossy tiles. Perhaps he came here to seek consolation for his unhappy love for Cassandre Salviati, the beautiful hostess of Talcy.

The château of Talcy rises from a rather austere plain, some kilometers away from there: a rugged château with its high square keep and its imposing façade. But its ruggedness is merely an appearance, because the walls enclose an exquisite grey and pink inner courtyard with an old well, a vegetable garden and a flower garden which lends itself to confidences and lovers' sighs.

The master of the house, Bernard Salviati, was a rich Florentine merchant who lived at Blois. In 1520, he obtained royal permission to fortify Talcy, 'with walls, towers, crenellations, barbicans, loopholes, machicolations, a draw bridge and other defensive equipment which is part of a fortress'. Such military paraphanalia might seem a little ridiculous if it did not reveal the merchant's desire to forget his humble origins. Moreover, the royal edict confirmed that the owner of the place could, under no circumstances, declare himself 'lord of the château, or have the right of guard'.

Bernard Salviati had four children, one of whom was a daughter of great beauty, Cassandre. On April 21, 1545, the banker gave an important banquet — at Blois or Talcy?—which the king honoured with his presence. Cassandre sang, accompanying herself on a guitar and the young clerk Pierre de Ronsard was dazzled to the extent of losing his reason: 'I saw her, I got mad about her', he confessed a little while later and for her he wrote the 183 sonnets, *Amours:*

Dedans un pré je vis une naïade
Qui comme une fleur
Marchait dessus les fleurs
Et mignotait un bouquet de couleurs,
Échevelée en simple vertugade.
Dès ce jour-là ma raison fut malade.

Alas, Cassandre was indifferent to him and their meetings at Talcy, beside the old well or beneath the cool shade of the arcaded gallery, suddenly came to an end. The young girl married shortly afterwards a certain Jean de Peigné, seigneur de Pray and Ronsard found other muses.

Did Agrippa d'Aubigné imagine he would be happier than Ronsard when he met Cassandra's niece, the beautiful Diane de Salviati? In truth, everything separated the two young people: Agrippa was a confirmed Protestant, marked by his father's death and the massacres at Amboise. Diane was Catholic. And yet they loved each other. After the Saint-Bartholomew massacres, the poet took refuge at Talcy, but when marriage was talked about, the young man was given to understand that he should give up all hope. He was deeply wounded and his violent poems, kept secret for a long time, gave vent to his anguish:

Diane, ta coutume est de tout déchirer
Enflammer, desbriser, ruiner,
Mettre en pièces, (...)
Diane, repens-toi, pense que tu as tort
Donner la mort à ceux qui te font
immortelle.

He wanted to die and his life was only saved thanks to the intervention of Ambroise Paré who trepanned him on a table in the château, after having anaesthetized him, it is said, with brandy

Hunting at Cheverny

At Cheverny we are once again in the residence of a great servant of State. The Hurault family were, from father to son, from Louis XII to Henri IV, secretaries, ministers and chancellors. For a long time, Cheverny was no more than a large fortress, of which nothing remains today apart from three pavilions in the servants' courtyard. The building which can be seen today, of a very pure classical style, was erected by Henri Hurault and dates from 1634. It was built after a very tragic story related in the 18th century, by one of the château owners, Durfort de Cheverny.

Henri Hurault belonged to Henri IV's retinue. He was a violent, ill-tempered, jealous man who kept his wife shut up—perhaps with reason— in his château. One day, Henri IV, teasing him and thinking he could not see, put his two fingers up to his head like two horns; the courtiers laughed, but Hurault saw his gesture in the mirror. Without a word, he left the room, jumped on his horse and galloped non-stop to Cheverny where he arrived at 5 o'clock. He had the gates opened and surprised a page in his wife's chamber who, on fleeing by the window, broke a leg. Hurault finished him off and sent for a priest. With a goblet in one hand and a pistol in the other, he entered his terrified wife's room. An hour later his wife died, she chose the poison. 'All this only took one morning' related the narrator, because Hurault was back at his post by the king at the end of the morning. But Henri IV did not much appreciate this kind of hurried justice and condemned his servant to exile.

Hurault was more fortunate with his second wife. Intelligent and thrifty, the young woman set about furnishing and decorating Cheverny according to the fashion of the day, using the most competent workmen of that time: the architect Boyer and the painter Jean Mosnier. She herself supervised the works. The original plan

A domain of thickets abounding with game, Cheverny wakes in the morning mist. The hunting party includes a whipper-in, two dog trainers, twenty horsemen with around eighty Anglo-French hounds, their colours are purple-red and royal blue.

of the château can be imagined behind the classical façade, but the corner towers which rose symmetrically on either side of the stairway have been transformed into important square pavilions.

Cheverny, like Brissac, Luynes, Sully and a few others, are numbered among the rare examples of châteaux which have remained in the same family for centuries. There was only a short fifty-year period at the end of the 18th century when the estate passed into the hands of a *famille de robe,* the Durfort family of Cheverny whose extravagant expenses at the court of Versailles obliged them to settle in the country. Then Cheverny came back to the Hurault family who, throughout the 19th century managed the estate as well as possible.

The present-day problems of keeping up a residence of this size are very different from those of the Ancien Régime. It still requires of course as much taste and care, but also a vast financial effort and knowledge of economics. From 1840, the Marquis de Vibraye, a descendant of the elder branch of the Hurault family, experimented with replanting the Sologne forest, thus anticipating the great organizing plans of Napoleon III. Today Cheverny draws its income mainly from agricultural developments, tourism and hunting. Modernism and tradition, the hunting parties at Cheverny continue, with an anachronism full of charm, to offer sacrifice to the god of the hunt.

When autumn tinges the ferns with gold, the sound of bugles and horns and the barking of dogs ring out. A gay group of horsemen wearing red coats and velvet hats rides out into the forest. A long knife tightly encased in its sheath dangles from the belt of one of the riders. The ladies are also dressed in red. At the sound of the hounds—there are seventy of them—they fly off on the scent of the stag; sometimes they gallop for hours until the animal is exhausted. It knows numerous ways of losing its scent, crossing a tarred road or a railway bank or a river is enough. At last, panting and wounded, it comes to a standstill. One stroke of the knife suffices and the entrails are given to the hounds while the master of hunt blows the horn of victory.

The hunting museum of Cheverny is like a graveyard with its two hundred trophies, and these cruel rituals, a bloody parade of a past age can be criticized, and yet hunting does not only serve pleasure or beauty. The excess livestock has to be reduced and preference is given to an aging male or a mal-formed animal. Moreover, the hunting parties do not make a kill on each occasion: the deer have a one in three chance of escaping and roe deer three out of four. The number of hunts is calculated in relation to the number of animals. And if susceptible people talk of cruelty, how much more murderous is the practice of beating for shooting parties!

The Marquise de Pompadour beautifies Menars

What brought Mme de Pompadour to Menars? Was it to find consolation among the resplendent landscape? A retreat to the wooded arbours, the temperate climate of the Loire valley? In 1762, she is no longer quite the triumphant favourite: at forty, the terrible exhaustion of court life, her travels and poisonous attacks by her enemies have ruined her health and beauty. And, above all, the main reason for her sadness, the king only visits her on rare occasions now, retained by affairs of state or perhaps some brunette beauty encountered in the forest of Marly...

La Pompadour has a weak heart. In spite of her doctor's advice, she obstinately continues to lead a hectic life in order to please her beloved, attending ceremonies and going on journeys. And always this passion for building and restoring royal buildings! Two years before, in 1760, she exchanged Menars with the king, for a residence she owned in Passy. From this rectilinear building, built in a rather severe

Painted by Boucher,
La Pompadour is radiant
in her triumphant beauty.
When she retired to Menars,
she no longer reigned completely
over the heart of her beloved king.

Preceding double page :
the apartments at Cheverny were beautifully decorated and are in a splendid state of conservation: 'nothing could be more gallant, convenient, more superb than the interior' wrote the Grande Mademoiselle *even then! The ceiling and panelling in the 'king's chamber' were painted by Mosnier and the bed was covered with Persian silk fabric.*

*The little temple, a rotunda,
to the west of the château de Menars
is by Soufflot,
who added a fore-part to the façade
including a ground floor
covered with a terrace,
he converted the Italian-style roofs
to the French style.
The little temple
is the only building which remains
of the 'manufactures'* (fabriques)
so much appreciated at this time.

style by Guillaume Charron, in 1637, Gabriel was to design for her a château full of grace, with two wings, four pavilions and a park dedicated to love. Every third month her carriage transports her with a noisy crowd of followers. She gives banquets and spends enormous sums which empty the treasury and increase the hostility of her enemies.

And she does not lack enemies. One young Parisian bourgeoise, born Antoinette Poisson and raised to the position of marchioness through Louis XV's favours, has often been accused of wastefulness and extravagant spending. On the banks of the Loire, this royal and profligate favourite

*The art of living
in the age of Enlightenment:
the gardens at Menars,
gently sloped down in terraces
towards the Loire,
were arranged by Mme de Pompadour,
then by her brother Marigny
according to the plans of Le Nôtre
or Jean-François Neufforge.
The collection of vases and statues
brought together by Marigny
to decorate the park
were dispersed his death.*

follows the Valois traditions. She is hated and laughed at; 'Cotillon IV', Frederick II ironically calls her. And local people do not scruple to write songs about her when she crosses the Loire over the new bridge at Orléans, built by Hugot and considered not very strong:

'Critics, Hugot is avenged
His brave bridge has carried
the heaviest load of France.'

But beauty and art plead in favour of La Pompadour. She gives artists the possibility to profit from royal lavishness; she gets the Direction des Bâtiments for her brother, Marquis de Marigny. Moreover, it was Marigny who inherited Menars and made the improvements which are visible today: the terraced gardens overlooking the Loire, the lime-tree drive, the grotto which serves as a background to a square lake. Soufflot replaced Gabriel. To facilitate the passage from one pavilion to another, a covered gallery was built, the Marigny gallery, as well as a subterranean corridor which made it possible to bring over dishes on a trolley equipped with an oven. Marigny had taste: 'On no account do I want modern chicory', he exclaimed. Tasteful, but not always tactful, he was accused of having taken beams and sculptures from abandoned royal châteaux, such as Blois to embellish Menars. □

from Blois to Tours

the garden of France

TOURAINE IS A MEETING PLACE for rivers and streams: the Indre, Vienne, Creuse, Cisse, Brenne, Bresme, Choisille, etc. Rising in the Auvergne mountains or the northern plains, they converge to deposit rich alluvium and nourish the famous 'varennes', game reserves of Touraine, ideal for market gardening. 'Shame on him who does not admire my joyous, beautiful and gallant Touraine with its seven valleys flowing with water and wine!', exclaimed Balzac. And yet it must not be forgotten that a few kilometers away from these valleys flowing with milk and Gâtinais honey, lie the Champeigne and the plain of Sainte-Maure, harsh lands that are difficult to cultivate.

Hillocks border the Loire from Blois to Tours, sometimes gently sloping down to catch the sun on their sides, laden with ripe Vouvray grapes, at others real cliffs of white micaceous chalk riddled with troglodyte dwellings. Amidst lines of poplars, the river flows gracefully and washes many islands—have they ever been counted? —sprinkled with bushes and clumps of vegetation. Towns and villages grew up naturally in the mild air, with their sloping roof-tops nestling beneath castle walls.

Chaumont: a royal barter

The large overhanging watch turrets of Chaumont draw a frontier line between Touraine and Blésois. The powerful mass of the château firmly set on a rock, is intimidating at first sight. But we must not be deceived by our first impression because the Renaissance has brought its civilizing influence to everyday customs and softened the edges. Around 1475, at the time when Charles d'Amboise was rebuilding his fortress, peace seemed durable and a greater accent was laid on decoration. The walls lost their thickness, the crenellations were embellished and mouldings, foliated scrolls and rosettes adorned the entrance gate to the spiral staircase. If the west tower and its adjacent wing still conjure up the sieges of war, the symmetrical south-east wing, of a later date (c. 1515),

Tranquillity, gentleness and nonchalance: this is where the garden of France begins. From Chaumont, built like a medieval castle on the summit of a steep slope, the view spreads over the marshlands where the Loire meanders between borders of poplars and clumps of willow.

pierced by numerous casement windows, was designed for the enjoyment of life.

And yet the hosts of Chaumont did not display much desire to make it their home. Catherine de Medicis, who bought the château from the Amboise family in 1550 for 120,000 *livres,* did not have her monogram engraved there, unlike her forbears. From her point of view, Chaumont was above all a source of income and a profitable one at that: 5,000 *livres* per annum. The queen rarely frequented the château, although sightseers today may visit her bedchamber furnished with a beautiful canopied bed and decorated with rich tapestries. Or perhaps she made some mysterious stay there in the company of that cunning Italian, Cosimo Ruggieri, who could read the future in a magic mirror. Did Ruggieri really conjure up the figures of her husband Henri II and his sons, François, Charles and Henri, on the terraces at Chaumont under the veiled light of the moon, and foresee the number of years they still had to live? Brantôme is adamant, but it is true that wherever the Florentine passes, chronicles speak of astrology and poison in connection with her.

In fact, if Queen Catherine did visit Chaumont, it was with the clear intention of inspecting her residence before making it over to Diane de Poitiers. Chaumont for Chenonceaux: this was the exchange offered to the beautiful mistress of Henri II. The Medicis family had retained the instincts of a family of bankers and merchants! These two women who mutually hated one another, the legal wife and the favourite mistress, for once came to an understanding or at least made an arrangement. In truth, Diane was scarcely in a position to refuse the queen's offer, as she has lost all power since the death of Henri II at the bloody tournament of Tournelles in January 1559. She was forced to give back the jewels Henri had given her and Catherine forbade her access to the court. Hate and wait: the Medicis motto is well known. Above all, the queen laid claim to Chenonceaux, but the affair was not easy to settle as Diane had taken all kinds of legal precautions when she acquired the estate. So, failing the means to enforce, a compromise was made: on May 10, 1560, an exchange deed was signed at Chinon. Diane de Poitiers became lady of Chaumont (her addorsed initials can be seen on the base of the parapet walk) and the dowager queen became sovereign ruler at Chenonceaux. It was a financially advantageous exchange for Diane de Poitiers, but she was not at ease in the medieval-looking fortress and made no attempts to improve it.

While the two ladies settled their differences, the court of the new king, the young François II, moved from Blois to Amboise. François II who was only seventeen was married to the most charming of princesses, Mary Stuart, two years his elder, and they were both very much in love. In the round, slightly puffy face of the young man, traces of a weak and lazy nature could be detected, but also the signs of the infectious disease which was soon to cause his death. It was, in fact, his doctors who sent him to Blois to be looked after and to enable him to profit from the better climate. But as Blois was full of the foul air of plots the small court decided to move to Amboise; François II ran no risks in this stronghold overlooking the Loire.

The king's favourites are goddesses! The prettiest among them, Diane de Poitiers, asked le Primatice to paint her like Diana, the huntress.

*The site of Amboise,
perched on a rock between the Loire
and the Amasse,
is remarkably good.
The large Minim Tower,
the high supporting walls
only seem to exist to emphasize
the flamboyant arcades,
pinnacles
and open-work balustrades
of the Renaissance façade.*

*The inner courtyard of Chaumont
barely conjures up
the austerity of the Middle Ages.
The east and south wings,
to the right and left
of the entrance gate,
were built between 1500 and 1515,
and much restored since then;
in the 18th century,
the suppression of the north wing
overlooking the Loire
opened up a magnificient view.*

Amboise: an accident by the tennis courts

Amboise, like Blois, was also a royal residence. This fortress, confiscated from the unruly counts of Amboise, had been attached to the crown in 1434. Fortified and strengthened, it provided shelter for the family of Louis XI while he was fighting the Burgundians.

It is not easy to imagine what the château was like before the alterations made by Charles VIII. Probably a very uncomfortable dwelling which benefited from one of the most attractive views over the Loire and where the modest Charlotte de Savoie, the wife of Louis XI, lived a retired life. The infant Dauphin, Charles, was baptized there in 1418 and grew up with his young fiancée Anne of Brittany.

On becoming king, Charles VIII attempted to modernize his childhood abode by extending the château to the east beyond the ditch which separated it from the hill: a grandiose project which led the Florentine ambassador to declare that Amboise resembled a city. In fact the building went on for years, from 1492 to 1497; work went on even at night under torchlight. In the meantime Charles VIII and Anne of Brittany, married in 1491, inhabited the ancient castle.

The first building to be completed was the *Logis des Sept vertus,* no longer extant today. It is known to have included a gallery which supported two storeys with mullion windows overlooking the valley of the Amasse. They housed the royal apartments which were provided with dressing-rooms and had windows of historiated stained glass. It is said that Queen Anne, who was concerned about hygiene, was the first to introduce the 'bath room'. Three enormous kitchens occupied the ground floor.

The second building, called the *Logis du roi* overlooks the Loire. It is a majestic, harmonious construction; now restored, it includes a low hall with heavy archways

'The towers of Amboise', relates Commynes, 'are so spacious that carts, mules and palanquins can climb up with ease'. Beneath its ogival vaults, the ramp of the Minim Tower rolls round in a gentle slope for over six hundred feet. Its diameter measures around nineteen yards. From the top, there is a very beautiful view over the Loire.

The Salle des États, *in the king's lodgings at Amboise, is separated into two naves by four slender pilasters decorated with* fleur de lys *and ermine and heated by a high fireplace bearing the arms of France and Britanny. Abd el-Kader who was kept prisoner here, divided it up with several partitions.*

There is no doubt that Flemish artists carved this stone gem, the chapel of Saint Hubert at Amboise, projecting from the rock and supported by a stone foundation. The porch lintel portrays the legends of Saint Christopher and Saint Hubert, while in the wide arch Anne of Brittany and Charle VIII kneel at the foot of the Virgin.

and, on the upper floor, an immense state room composed of two Gothic style naves and lit by large windows. At the end of either building, two enormous towers provide access to the Minim tower (on the Loire side) and the Hurbault tower (on the south side) which encloses a three metres wide staircase, up which not only horses but carts can climb. The chapel of Saint Hubert, used as the queen's oratory, is a gem of Gothic architecture, linked to the château by low buildings.

Building work was not interrupted by the Italian expedition in 1494. Although the construction was too far advanced for the plans to be altered, the king dreamed of reproducing the marvellous gardens which enchanted him at Naples. The gardener Dom Pacello designed the beds planted with apple, pear and orange trees arranged in neat rectangles and surrounded by a painted trellis; on the Loire side a gallery shields the garden from the wind and, in the middle, an octagonal shaped pavilion topped with a cupola encloses a fountain.

Amboise was the birthplace of what one may call for the first time a court. The suite of Charles VIII had four times as many followers as that of his father Louis XI and the royal palace was the scene for hitherto unknown luxury. The account books show that the extremely rich furnishings included magnificent tapestries from Flanders and France, Turkish carpets, forty-five double beds, each with twelve sets of sheets, hangings, bed canopies, damask, silk and satin curtains. The plate was of solid silver decorated with the monogram of Anne of Brittany, the Franciscan girdle; the furniture included about fifty sculptured chests, as many tables, dressing tables and red leather-backed chairs. We know that the king's bedchamber was hung with yellow and red.

At Amboise, the royal day started with mass. Then Charles VIII conferred with his secretaries and close friends. He liked to surround himself with humanists, painters, orators and poets. The court was the centre of elegance, at least on feast days: the king was dressed in violet and white with an ermine-lined coat; the fashion was for stripes, feathers and square-toed slippers. The afternoon was devoted to open air activities, principally hunting: the stables were full of magnificent stallions and palfreys. Falcons were reared in an immense aviary and the king was passionately fond of his three greyhounds who used even to follow him into his chamber. Two tennis courts were constructed, one to the south of the garden, the other in the old ditch near the keep. The evenings were spent in playing parlour games, cards and dice.

The king and queen did not spend the entire year at Amboise; they left their children there: the young Dauphin Charles-Orland was supervised by a tutor and a hundred guards kept watch from the château gates. But unfortunately they could not guard against epidemics and smallpox, which was raging in the surrounding countryside, struck down the infant, aged three, in 1495. The following three children lived

only a few days, the last child being a little girl who died in 1498.

1498: what a sad year! On April 7, on the eve of Palm Sunday, Charles VIII leaves his chamber with the queen to go and watch the tennis in the château ditch. The royal couple pass through a gallery called the Haquelebac gallery, overlooking the playing ground. This gallery was, in effect, a disagreeable place, in a poor state of repair: 'Everyone urinated in it' wrote Commynes who relates the incident. As he walks along, the king cracks his head against the lintel of a door and, although somewhat dazed, he continues his way, watches the players and jokes with one or other of the onlookers. On this eve of Palm Sunday, he even confides that he has a 'great desire never to commit either a mortal or venial sin'. But as he utters these words he falls backwards, speechless. The courtiers all rush to his side but nobody dares to move him and he remains there for hours lying on a straw mattress in the corridor open to the wind. On three occasions he manages to say a few words to his confessor and at eleven in the evening he expires. Was it concussion? It is highly probable, although some historians attribute his sudden death to poison.

Anne of Brittany is prostrate with grief. In seven years of married life, she had seen three of her children die, followed by her husband, and she is only twenty-two. She refuses to don white, the colour of mourning and orders black costumes. She is in tears when she receives the emissary of the new king, Louis d'Orléans, now Louis XII, who was already devising a plan to annul his marriage and oblige the inconsolable widow to take a husband.

Leonardo da Vinci at Amboise

The death of Charles VIII put an immediate stop to work on Amboise. Louis XII preferred Blois, his childhood residence, where he took Anne of Brittany, now his wife, as soon as possible. Abandoned by the court,

Charles VIII and Anne of Britanny made Amboise the principal great royal residence. More liberal than intelligent, fascinated by the brilliance of Italian civilization, the young king claimed to the crown of Naples through the hazards of inheritance. His successors were to be equally fascinated by the 'Italian mirage'. Although conquests were short-lived, the 'Italian fashion' was long lasting.

Amboise became the residence of the heir to the throne, François d'Angoulême, and his mother, Louise de Savoie. François was then engaged to the young Claude, the eldest daughter of Anne of Brittany who continually pushed back the wedding date in the hope of giving birth to an infant dauphin and make this marriage unnecessary. But at thirty-seven, mother of two girls, and worn out by fruitless pregnancies, she passed away on January 9, 1514.

Nothing now stood in the way of the marriage between Claude of France and François of Angoulême, the heir to the crown. It was a gloomy ceremony, Louis XII having forbidden any celebrations or pomp. The bridal couple were dressed in black — a symbol of constancy. A few months later, the old king also died, and François ascended the throne, at the age of twenty. Before leaving for the wars in Italy he gave magnificent feasts at Amboise. Full of spirit and loving luxury, he could not stay long in one place. He moved constantly, followed by his 'little gang' from château to château, hunt to hunt, and, before long, from mistress to mistress. But he was kept at Amboise by his admiration and friendship for the ageing Leonardo da Vinci, with whom he loved to discuss great architectural projects.

After the victory of Marignano, François visited the great artist and, for the sum of 4,000 ducats, brought the Mona Lisa back to France. He even persuaded the Italian master to leave his native country, where the rival star of Michelangelo was beginning to rise, and to come back with him to the banks of the Loire, in return for an annual pension of 700 *écus.* Leonardo accepted the offer.

Leonardo was sixty seven when he arrived in Touraine in the spring of 1516, accompanied by his pupil Francesco Melzi and two servants; he was by now an ageing and exhausted man. The king welcomed him personally, taking him in his arms. He had had a charming residence prepared for him, a little way from the château; the manor of Cloux — or the Clos-Lucé — which had formerly belonged to a follower of Louis XI and which was bought back by Charles VIII. Anne of Brittany and the little Charles Orland often used to go there through the Lion Gate. Then the manor was used by the sister of François I, Marguerite of the Marguerites, as a country retreat; it was here that she wrote her first poems, before *The Heptameron.* With its pink brick, octagonal turret and its white stone oratory where Anne of Brittany used to come and weep for her dead children, the Clos-Lucé was a modest but captivating residence which pleased Leonardo. And no doubt the artist found, in the distant misty blues of the Loire valleys something of the sweetness of his gentle Florentine hills.

The 15th century manor of Clos-Lucé houses a Leonardo da Vinci Museum where one can see fifty models of machines built after the masters' sketches. Leonardo ended his days here, close to the mysterious smile of the Mona Lisa *from which he could not be parted.*

Leonardo da Vinci dominated his age. When François I brought him to France, he did not only welcome the greatest artist of his time, but the finest engineer of the century: his researches dealt with architecture, hydraulics, metallurgy and textiles...

In spite of his age and the rheumatism which had stiffened his hand, the master continued to work. He organised magnificent illuminations for the king at the Clos-Lucé where, at night, 'it was as bright as day'. He studied the projects for purifying the Sologne and cutting a canal which was to pass through Romorantin; he drew up plans for a sort of helicopter and constructed a model lion which was so lifelike that it terrified the court ladies! He was tirelessly active, however it is not known whether the frescoes in the oratory were executed by him or by his pupil.

In 1519 the winter was so severe that the Loire froze, and when the ice broke up it carried away one of the arches of the bridge at Amboise. The artist rescued a swallow, which he fed and which became his companion. This was his last winter, and he died on May 2nd. He was buried with great ceremony in the collegiate chapel of Saint Florentin at the château of Amboise — which was later destroyed. A stone slab in the chapel of Saint Hubert protects his remains, which were removed there under the Second Empire.

Corpses hanging from balconies

Under the reign of Henri II and Catherine de Medicis, Amboise remained a royal residence for the children. The walled garden and the pure air, due to the elevated position of the château, made it a peaceful, protected spot. The young princes were brought up with companions of their own age; they had their own house, a retinue of servants, nursemaids, apothecaries, doctors and launderesses. Their parents made frequent visits or sent their portraits. Only the heir, the Dauphin François, did not reside at Amboise as he was obliged to follow the royal suite in order to learn the art of kingship. He was sixteen in 1559 when his father died and he became King François II.

At that time, the country was in the throes of the tragic Wars of Religion. Huguenots were burnt at Beaugency and Chinon. With the death of Henri II the real power belonged to the House of Guise who manipulated the young king and encouraged further persecution of the Protestants. The situation became so critical that Protestant nobles, pushed to the extreme, decided to remove François II from under the influence of the Guise faction and resolved to kidnap him. But the court got wind of the plot and left Blois in haste for Amboise in March 1560. To create a diversion, a masked ball was given in the château. From behind their masks, the armed servants kept their eyes open.

The tragic ending to the story is well known. The plot was discovered. Caught in a trap, the conspirators were captured in their hiding places, either at the château de Noisay between Tours and Amboise, or in the forest of Château-Renault. La Renaudie, their leader, was killed by a shot from an arquebus and his quartered body was hung up in pieces on the gates of Amboise. Then followed the terrible massacres of the prisoners, the most fearful punishment: death by drowning, hanging, decapitation. Gallows were set up in the courtyard. Some conspirators were hanged from the balcony and crenellations overlooking the Loire. They hung there for several hours and the young royal couple appeared at the window to look at the spectacle. The peasants, Catholics and Protestants alike, were terrified. Among the spectators stood a little six years old boy, Agrippa d'Aubigné, whose father had brought there to swear vengeance for the death of his brothers in religion. For several days afterwards, bodies floated down the Loire.

The royal couple did not linger much longer at Amboise after the massacres and when they left it was never to return. The ill-fated fortress was often used as a prison and its last famous captive was to be Abd el-Kader.

Chinoiserie on the Loire at Chanteloup

Three kilometers away from Amboise, one can scarcely believe one's eyes: on the outskirts of the forest a strange obelisk, divided into seven parts which fit into one another, is reflected in a pool: this is the chinese pagoda of Chanteloup, the only remains of the magnificent residence which was the home of the duc de Choiseul during his disgrace.

The exiled minister of Louis XV reconstructed a miniature Versailles at Chanteloup, which the entire court came to see, much to the fury of the king and Mme Du Barry, instigator of the affair. The Duchess of Grammont and the Duke of Orléans both had their own apartments there. The collections of engravings and rare books were a delight for guests. They did not meet in the morning but at three o'clock 'dinner' was served in the apartments or could also be taken with their hosts. The splendour and vastness of the château was such that Durfort de Cheverny, a guest from the neighbourhood, took twenty minutes to walk from the grand hall to his chamber. Hunting, of course, was one of the most popular recreations in the beautiful forest that spread out close at hand; twice a week deer were hunted; and the game was shared out in one of the courtyards to the south of the château. The stables were full of an impressive number of cows and pigs, enough to feed an entire population. Although the day was not regulated by any formal protocol, guests were expected to dress in the evening as if at court, with the ladies wearing hooped dresses. Backgammon, billiards and lively conversation lasted until midnight, sometimes a sumptuously illuminated ball was given, worthy of Versailles.

The Chinese pagoda was a monument erected to the memory of friends in exile. Visitors' names were engraved on the stone. The little 'folly', built by Camus, cost nearly 40,000 crowns. Was it this kind of extravagant expense which caused Mme de Choiseul, on the death of her husband, to exclaim: 'Good God, give me time to pay my husband's debts'?

Chanteloup was destroyed during the Restoration by the 'black gangs' of property dealers who dismantled it stone by stone. Nothing remains except for the front pavilion and the pagoda where Anatole France liked to wander so much. □

The Renaissance customs were cruel: the conspirators of Amboise were beheaded, drowned, quartered or hung from the balconies of the château which ornamented the windows of the Salle des États; the young king and his wife watched the scene from a window.

a walk along the Cher: Chenonceaux

Philibert Delorme boldly spanned the Cher with these robust but graceful arches. The three 'sections' of the château can be clearly seen: the isolated Marques tower, the Bohier château and its extension, the gallery lying across the river built for Catherine de Medicis which crowns the bridge of Diane de Poitiers.

As it flows from the Berry, the Cher river cuts its way between the troglodyte slopes of Bourré and the hills planted with vineyards and pine trees. Severe at first, it grows milder the closer it comes to the Touraine and nearer the royal river, the Loire, to whom it pays its tribute: a peaceful river, held in check by dams along part of its course, which has encouraged industry; 'a bourgeois river', it has been called, which seems 'to exist as much for its usefulness as for its pleasure, like prose after poetry' (H. Guerlin).

The Cher is first and foremost the river of Chenonceaux, the château of Diane de Poitiers, photographed and admired a hundred times over, a picture postcard of France. But Chenonceaux (it used to be spelt Chenonceau) retains memories of the time when it was a mill, a busy fortified mill which the Cher worked for the Marques family. The attractive tower (remodelled) and the foundations of the front archway are important remains from this period.

In 1515, the architect Trinqueau began to build the château. Chenonceaux is a happy château, built for entertainment, which brings to mind pleasant pictures of banquets and balls, rather than plots or massacres. Moreover, its successive owners — always female — put so much love and care into its decoration that they could only be removed by coercion and force and always with great sadness.

The inhabitants of Tours come to Savonnières to make a good catch of fish. All around, well-kept vineyards spread out along the slopes and grottos full of stalactites called caves-gouttières *are cut out of the chalk stone.*

The first owners to suffer such setbacks in fortune were the Counts of Marques: in order to pay their debts, they were obliged to transfer Chenonceaux to a man who was then on the way up, Thomas Bohier, royal tax collector. The affair could not be settled without wrangling and dragged on for years; it was only in 1512 that Bohier and his wife, Catherine Briçonnet, became the real owners, at a price of 12,450 *livres,* of the Chenonceaux estate which they raised to the state of castellany.

Catherine Briçonnet, from one of the leading families of Touraine, was an up-to-date woman, she undertook the supervision of the works and spent her time and fortune on making improvements and modernising the Marques home. A gracious manor house rose in place of the old mill: a square two-storeyed building flanked with corbelled turrets on either side and resting on two old pillars set in the bed of the Cher. The forecourt around a bailey disappeared, as did the inconvenient spiral staircase, but in their place four large rooms opening on either side of a hall and a straight balustraded flight of stairs of Italian design. The wide windows were set with pilasters, the kitchens housed in the foundation mass, with a small staircase leading to a sort of floating bridge over the Cher where provisions could be unloaded. Building work went on right until 1521, the date of the consecration of the chapel. The king then authorized the construction of a bridge over the Cher to facilitate removal of the debris, but Catherine died in 1523, before she could see the project through.

Her heir, Antoine Bohier, was unable to continue the work: the Bohier family were involved in the disgrace of the financier Semblançay and ruined. They had to refund 190,000 *livres* to the Touraine treasury; unable to pay, they offered Chenonceaux, by way of compensation, and François I was attracted by the idea of acquiring 'this beautiful site and home, well placed in an agreable countryside'. He went there four or five times to hunt.

It was during one of his brief visits that the Dauphin, the future Henri II and his wife, Catherine de Medicis, discovered this superb residence on the Cher river. His favourite, Diane de Poitiers, widow of the comte de Brézé in 1531, was a member of the party. A semi-official *ménage à trois* with all the dramas that such a situation implied; Catherine, the loving wife of her indifferent husband, jealous and deceived, swallowed her humiliation and constantly played the comedy of friendship, she even pretended to show regard for her lucky rival in order to retain the king's favour! Diane, still a superb woman although nearing

D'or au lion d'argent
et un chef de gueule!
the arms of Thomas Bohier,
a financier who grew rich
under three kings
and who took for his motto:
'S'il vient à point me souviendra'.
Alas, not everything
came at the right moment
for the bankrupt treasurer.

Catherine,
appreciated by François I,
ıt held in low esteem by the court
who considered her birth
unworthy of the royal family,
bided her time
with patience and determination.
She knew how to wait,
as nine years passed
before she gave birth to the first
of her ten children!

hen the beautiful Diane de Poitiers
st her husband, Louis de Brézé
1531,
ançois I entrusted the education
his son Henri, then aged twelve,
her.
veral year later
e became his mistress
though twenty years his senior.

forty, reigned with all her beauty and reputation: a white throat, broad shoulders which emphasized the slimness of her waist, her magnificient hair held back under a black hood, permanently dressed in black and white, which gave her that imposing and maternal air and which so delighted her royal lover, twenty years her junior. Portraits by Jean Goujon and François Clouet have immortalized her flawless nudity and, undoubtedly, this was how Henri II pictured her, immune to the scars of time.

But this goddess was nonetheless a business woman. Henri refused her nothing. He had her monogram, a crescent moon, carved on the façade of the Louvre and in his royal palaces; he gave her jewelry, lands and gifts which today would be estimated at millions of francs. On becoming king in 1547, he made her a gift of Chenonceaux which had been crown property since 1535. An illegal gift as the royal estates were inalienable; so his covetous mistress had to find a clause enabling her to find fault with the transaction signed by the Bohier family in 1535. A way out was soon found, the unfortunate Bohier was persuaded that he had overestimated the value of his estate and the sale was declared void. The château was put up for sale by auction and Diane quite simply bought it back — with money from the royal treasury, it goes without saying! On June 8, 1555, the favourite was at last recognized as rightful owner to an estate where she had, for several years, undertaken large-scale work. Long may she profit from it! Five years later fate was to upset her well-laid plans.

Diane de Poitiers, capable woman that she was, put the accounts in order; she kept a close watch on farm rents and the sale of wine and wheat. She was in urgent need of money because she wanted to complete the construction of a bridge over the Cher, for which Philibert Delorme has drawn up plans. Besides, the building was proceeding at a very slow pace and was to cost 9,000 *livres* even before completion. Diane also gave all her attention to her gardens to make them a temple worthy of love: green bowers, rare lilies, rose bushes sent to her by the archbishop of Tours, flowerbeds laid out in the Italian fashion... utility and pleasure were combined with the planting of a hundred and fifty mulberry bushes for

Jean Goujo[n] carved the monumental fireplac[e] in the Diane de Poitiers's chambe[r]. The intertwined initia[ls] of the favourite and Henri [II] ornament the mantlepiec[e] as well as the wall[s]

The chamber of Catherine de Médicis, on the first floor of the Bohier wing, is still sumptuously furnished with a canopy bed and decorated with tapestries. The queen also had a study on the ground floor, the Cabinet Vert, whose ceiling remained intact for five centuries.

the silkworms; the vineyards were tenderly cared for, but one day the rising Cher swept away the dikes and flooded the park. The garden was immediately replanted. Fortunately Henri II made his contribution by granting Diane a pension of 5,500 *livres* in recompense for 'the good, pleasant and commendable services which the said lady has rendered our dear and much loved companion, the Queen'. An understatement which surely delighted Catherine!

In 1559, the gallery over the bridge and the conversion of the right bank still remained to be completed. The accidental death of Henri II upset all these plans; Diane was obliged to surrender Chenonceaux and she retired to Anet where Brantôme was to describe her as a still splendid woman even when over sixty years of age.

Licentious festivities

Catherine was, at long last, mistress of the realm; she now occupied the place of which Diane's brilliance had deprived her. 'Her court, wrote Brantôme, was truly an earthly paradise and a school of beauty.' She surrounded herself with the most beautiful ladies of France, the young ladies of the Flying Squadron, who came from the best families in the kingdom. She gave concerts in her apartments 'open to all well educated people'; her furniture is painted with gay colours, gold sparkles on cushions, on mouldings and panels and on the ladies gowns. No one knew better than Catherine, how to give magnificent receptions and balls and she did not stint herself at Chenonceaux to prove before the entire world that she was queen.

The occasion for the first of these receptions was the arrival of the young king François II and his wife, Mary Stuart at Chenonceaux on March 31, 1560. The court has just left the sinister château d'Amboise after the massacres and, along the route, the local people line up to watch the procession pass by, waving flags and beating drums. Triumphal arches and plaster statues have transformed the château into some antique paradise: two young girls, representing Victory and Fame, await at the entrance while a helmeted Pallas recites complimentary verses from a balcony. In the evening, clusters of light illuminate the pathways, and fireworks explode into a shower of multicoloured stars over the flowerbeds. There is tilting at the ring, hunting and tennis. But the humid climate of the Cher is unhealthy for François and, a few days later, the court withdraws to Tours.

Three years later in April 1563, Chenonceaux was to welcome Charles IX who succeeded François II, carried off by an infected mastoid. Once again there was a tremendous display of luxury and wealth possibly on an even grander scale. Charles, who had reached the age of thirteen, opened the ball with his sister Marguerite. The young ladies of the Flying Squadron, dressed as nymphs in silver veils, sprang from the bushes and danced the Poitou *branle.* Then followed a boat excursion along the Cher to the sound of music. The following day the guests were requested to arrive disguised as shepherds, dressed in white satin, for a masked ball. Refreshments were served in the park by the ladies of the Flying Squadron then, in the evening a contest was held between

On the right bank of the Cher,
Diane de Poitiers
laid out the gardens
which still bear her name;
but the flowerbeds
which can be seen today
are different from the stretches of green
where the favourite
liked to walk with the king.
Catherine de Medicis transformed them
into Italian style flowerbeds.

fifty barges decorated with garlands of flowers. It was as if the court wanted to lose itself in amusements.

History also relates that Catherine stopped at Chenonceaux on several occasions in order to speed up the alterations supervised by Bernard Palissy; the gallery which spans the Cher had just been started. To her we owe the sumptuous flowerbeds filled with fountains streaming with water, the artificial grottos set in rockeries, the pools and ponds and an amphitheatre like some background to an antique dream.

The massacres of Saint-Bartholomew's Day in 1572 interrupted this sumptuous pomp and circumstance. Charles IX died next in 1574 and his successor was the most refined, immoral, irresolute and mystical member of the Valois dynasty. A man full of contradictions, undoubtedly his mother's favourite son, but ungrateful as so often are those too dearly cherished. He

showed as much inclination for a retreat to a monastery as for the most licentious of amusements; he sincerely thought of the good of his kingdom and yet sank the last resources of a country already bled to death into these dazzling festivities. He required the most formal protocol and yet his court was noted for its extravagant costume, its painted faces and provocative make-up.

On May 15, 1577, Henri III gave a reception at Plessis-lès-Tours which is still remembered, to reward his younger brother d'Alençon, who had just won a victory over the Huguenot stronghold. The guests were to arrive disguised, the men dressed up as women and vice versa. The following Sunday, Catherine was hostess at Chenonceaux in her turn for an extravagant reception. The king arrived disguised as a woman as for a masked ball, wearing a richly embroidered costume, with a low neckline, a frill and three rows of pearls adorning his throat. His favourite companions, powdered and curled, wore similar costumes. The banquet took place in the garden behind the Tour de Marques, near the foot of the rockery. The ladies of the Flying Squadron served 'half-naked with their hair flowing like a bride' relates Brantôme. Amongst the guests were a few frivolous beauties such as Charlotte de Beaune, Mme de Guicherville, the lady of Montsoreau whom we shall meet again later on in gallant company. The three queens were present, but whereas Louise de Vaudémont, the wife of Henri III was discreet and modest in her behaviour, her sister-in-law, Marguerite laughed coquettishly and took pleasure in these unseemly amusements. The banquet alone cost over à 100,000 *livres* which had to be raised on loan. Details of the festivities have been lost: maybe fireworks on the river banks, music, plays and perhaps less innocent

The châteaux of the Loire provided a sumptuous background for royal festivities which well-suited the decadent refinement of the court of Henri III. The ball given for the marriage of the Duc de Joyeuse with the Queen's sister, Marguerite de Navarre, cost the treasury over one million crowns!

Valençay was built around 1540 by Jacques d'Estampes who was inspired by Chambord in erecting this enormous central tower cut up by turrets, balanced by the superimposed pilasters. But the lantern dome, already classical in style, replaced the pepper-pots. The symmetrical west wing, of more modest dimensions, was added in the 17th century.

pastimes amid the convenient shadows of the poorly lit halls and behind bushes.

The reception seemed licentious and shocked contemporary onlookers, it was to be the last grand reception at Chenonceaux: its apotheosis. Catherine still paid several visits to the Cher valley, to supervise the completion of the two storey gallery designed by Philibert Delorme, but through lack of time and money, she was unable to complete all her plans, which were to have included magnificent buildings on the right bank. And this was a blessing as far as the balance and harmony of the château is concerned. More modestly, she had a few outbuildings erected for her retinue, topped with a framework in the shape of an imperial crown, the famous *dômes.*

Catherine bequeathed Chenonceaux to her daughter-in-law, the sweet Queen Louise: a discreet, faithful queen, who went there to mourn her dead husband: a white ghost wandering in a melancholy background. She had her bedchamber painted black with death heads on the ceiling; she never left her apartments and followed mass from her bed through a small window pierced in the wall of her chamber, until her death in 1601.

For two centuries the château lay hidden behind mist; awaiting its purchase in the 18th century by the *Fermier Général* Dupin to awake from a long sleep. The fifth lady of Chenonceaux, Mme Dupin, restored, replanted, entertained and surrounded herself with great minds. Jean-Jacques Rousseau, invited in 1747 as tutor to the young Dupin, was delighted with the place; he made music, acted in plays and wrote poetry: 'I became as fat as a monk', he confessed. It was certainly not amidst such delightful company that he could devote himself to solitary musings...

Chenonceaux sums up all to the charm of the Cher river. 'There is, I know not what kind of singular sweetness and aristocratic serenity which exudes from the château of Chenonceaux' wrote Flaubert. And yet, for those who wish to draw aside from the royal homes and explore the countryside, the Cher still holds surprises in store for them: the large square keep of Montrichard, the fortress of the feared Fulk III Nerra, Gué-Péan, a delightful hunting lodge of white and blue set in a small quiet valley, the ancient fortress of Selles reflected in the curve of the river, Saint-Aignan and, further away, the château of Valençay, magnificently set on vast terraces, bought by Talleyrand in 1803. But such treasures do not really belong to the Loire valley, let us return them to Berry. □

from Tours to Ussé . . .

Tours is a town
'inspired by the genius of the Loire'
(Boylesve).
The large Gothic nave
of the cathedral
guards the town to the east;
to the west
runs the maze of little streets
of the old town
from which rise turrets and bell towers.

a succession of castles

BETWEEN TOURS AND USSÉ, the Loire has almost reached its prime, swollen by the rivers Cher and Indre. Its wide arms encircle oblong-shaped islands covered with lush green osier bushes, its banks scattered with poplars and willows smell of sweet honeysuckle. The Loire is the most luxuriant river of France. Tiny villages warm their tiled roofs at the feet of castles. Along old battered bridges, one can easily imagine a line of horsemen in clinking armour. The countryside is peaceful, civilized, conducive to a stay in the country, a rural haven. Balzac spent some time at la Grenadière, a kilometre away from the bridge at Tours, and, Anatole France, another lover of the Loire, died at la Béchellerie near by.

History has arranged stopping places along this part of the river, with its towers set amidst straggling bushes where birds nest, ruined fortresses with grass-covered courtyards, proud castles. We must go in search of them after stopping off at Tours, where the old castle of the Guise family strikes an austere note in a town full of charm and grace. Here the young Prince de Joinville, emprisoned after the assassination of his father, the Duc de Guise, at Blois, leaped fifteen feet down into the ditch before fleeing along the river bank. It is here that the Loire is perhaps the best expression of the French countryside 'varied in its monotony, gentle, gracious with a beauty which enchants without captivating, charms without seducing and, in a word, has more common sense than greatness, and more wit than poetry', this was how Flaubert described it.

This 17th century water-colour shows us the lay-out of the château du Plessis-lès-Tours, of which only a fragment remains today, part of the wing of the royal lodgings can be reconstituted. A rectangle fifty metres by thirty-five, it resembles Le Plessis-Bourré, minus the corner towers. The king resided in the highest wing.

Plessis-lès-Tours: a charming residence

On leaving the town of Tours, one comes across a modest brick building flanked with an octagonal turret set in the flat suburbs in the midst of trees and market gardens: Plessis-lès-Tours, built on the Montil family estate. When compared with a royal château, there is nothing spectacular about it. Who could believe that behind these walls pierced with windows and brightened by a decorative chain of bricks lived a gloomy king, Louis XI, who has been immortalized with his Machiavellian face beneath a fur cap? In vain, one searches for cells and dungeons, dark corridors where his unhappy victims wander like ghosts: the only subterranean passage found was almost level with the ground floor, but legend dies hard and owes much to the talent of Walter Scott.

Plessis-lès-Tours, redecorated in 1477, was a surprisingly modern building for its age. Of course, fortifications with a drawbridge over the moat protected the castle and, according to the custom, the postern gate is flanked by two circular towers and leads into a forecourt filled with guard-posts. But the lordly dwelling is a comfortable and light-filled rose brick building: a glazed gallery makes access to the chapel dedicated to Saint Jean possible whatever the weather. From the first floor, there is a view over a beautiful park, with gardens and orchards and, in the far distance, the rooftops of Tours. The furniture, although not luxurious, was comfortable for the age: new tapestries, billiard tables, libraries and tubs for taking a bath.

Louis XI owned several other residences, but he felt at home at Plessis; he was to spend the last days of his life in this country retreat. He liked to hunt in the neighbouring game reserves; he wore a coarse woollen costume and entertained a few select guests in the evening, including his nephew Pierre de Beaujeu; the meals were savoury: capons, grouse, hedgehogs, storks, the horns of young deers cut into small pieces and fried in lard, with wine from Orléans and Bordeaux; a doctor kept an eye on the royal table.

Towards the end of his life, trembling with fear at approaching death, Louis XI

Of the spacious residence of Plessis-lès-Tours, only this royal lodge remains. It was in this room on the first floor with its brick walls decorated with stone, heated by a vast fireplace that Louis XI passed away.

This portrait of Louis XI was probably the work of Fouquet. Rather ugly, he was always seen wearing coarsely made clothes; here he wears the chain of the Order of Saint Michael of which he was the founder. Curious about everything and shrewd, Louis XI laid the foundations for the modern state.

became morbidly suspicious; he spied on every one, went to inspect the kitchens himself and had his servants replaced by new ones. His piety and devotion, an insurance for the next world became more intense; no means of protecting his life was neglected: he showered gifts on the churches, recited novenas to the glory of the Holy Virgin of Cléry, made a pilgrimage to Saint-Benoît, acquired relics and sent all the way to the far corners of Italy for the Calabrian hermit François de Paule. But all these prayers did not bring back his health. Fear oppressed him, so he added an iron railing around the all too vulnerable château, with pointed spikes criss-crossed in several places. Miradors were installed on the tops of the walls, soldiers mounted the guard with orders to fire on anything that moved, as soon as the drawbridge was pulled up.

The king was at the château when he suffered his first attack, which left him speechless. When he was somewhat recovered, he called for his son, the young Dauphin Charles, then aged thirteen, to give him his instructions and entrusted the regency to his daughter, Anne de Beaujeu. His remission was short-lived and he died on August 31, 1483 in the care of François de Paule.

The background of Plessis, modest and unspectacular, scarcely conjures up today these dark hours of French history, any more than it corresponds to the romantic picture painted by Walter Scott in *Quentin Durward.* Nonetheless, the château is a model for many other buildings in the Loire valley which have been kept in a much better state of repair. And as such, it is worth a visit.

One of these châteaux is Luynes, on the right bank of the Loire. The fortress belonged to the lord of Maillé from whom Louis XI brought the lands of the Montil family to build Plessis. Thanks to the sale, Maillé was able to modernize his home which he transformed into an exact replica of the royal residence, with the same brick walls, the same decoration of brick chains, the octagonal tower flanked at its summit by a smaller turret, the same and wide windows. But Luynes also bears the scars of time, so that the only vestige of the 15th century is the octagonal turret.

There is something striking about this massive, square building as it appears on the right bank when you approach from the west. Romantic from far off, the fortress grows grim when one draws near, and the four large towers which emerge from an expanse of greenery, have retained the power of a medieval fortress. During the 17th century the estate was elevated into a duchy and presented by Louis XIII to his favourite, Charles d'Albert de Luynes, as a reward for his having got rid of the domination of the Queen Mother, Marie de Medicis. Maillé became Luynes and the château remained in the hands of the same family for centuries.

A few kilometres from this beautiful, proud residence, the fate of the château de Cinq-Mars, seems all the more tragic in contrast; only a few topless towers remain above a village half-hidden in the rocky cliff.

The Duc de Luynes and the Marquis de Cinq-Mars met at the court of Louis XII, where they were both favourites, each in their own way. Indeed, who could resist the charm of this handsome man of twenty, Henri d'Effiat, Marquis de Cinq-Mars? His

Square in design, supported by solid buttresses, Luynes has retained a harsh military appearance; on the west side divided by four cylindrical towers, a brick building dating from the early Renaissance is set in the inner courtyard.

Cinq-Mars was sixteen when Louis XIII noticed his youthful beauty and took him into his service still almost a child. Six years later, because he tried to confront the all powerful Richelieu, this handsome but rather frivolous head fell on the scaffold.

portraits show him to be an attractive man with sparkling eyes below curled hair: noble features calculated to inspire the greatest of passions and worthy to serve as a romantic model for Alfred de Vigny's hero. As for being a hero, Cinq-Mars was above all, an elegant and frivolous man of society, who accumulated debts, enjoyed gaming, courted Marion Delorme and, was in no way fit for the aspirations of a serious minded and pious king. His brilliant ascent had gone to his head and blinded him to the rival power of Richelieu, which threatened his ambitions. He considered himself invulnerable and in order to get rid of the cardinal who stood in his way, he intrigued, encouraged Gaston d'Orléans to revolt and made treaties with Spain. The chance to break this insolent man was too good to be lost: he was accused of secret communication with the enemy and high treason! Richelieu refused to pardon him, and even the king was obliged to repudiate his friend, abandoning him to the revenge of his minister. Cinq-Mars was arrested, tried and beheaded on September 12, 1642; he died courageously. The towers of his castle were cut down in proportion to his infamy.

Langeais marks the frontier between Anjou and Touraine and this probably explains why this imposing fortress, symbol of the declining feudal system, was erected beside on the old square tower of Fulk III Nerra. Grey, gloomy and menacing, its mere presence had a deterrent effect; Louis XI had it built to protect his estate of Plessis-lès-Tours. The work was put in the charge of Jean Bourré, familiarly called *'mon compère'*. It is a paradox that this enormous, remarkably well conserved château was never a victim to siege or assault or any clumsy restoration and, with its rare collection of chests, and beds, it gives an accurate picture of every day life in the 15th century.

The only important historical event linked with this military monument is a wedding, and what a wedding! That of King Charles VIII and the young Anne of Brittany, which ratified the unification of Brittany and France. The ceremony was to take place during the month of December,

Situated at the confluence of the Loire and the Roumer, Langeais, like Luynes, is a château of the Middle Ages; one stands in admiration before the feeling of power and majesty of the château gateway, although the moats no longer exist.

but already early in the month the king settled there with his court; his fiancée, who came, probably by barge, from Nantes with an enormous trousseau, followed him shortly. On December 6, the engaged couple signed the marriage contract, drawn up by two notaries, after a solemn reading, it stipulated that if the king died without an heir Anne would marry his successor. This historical scene probably took place in the great hall on the first floor hung with sumptuous tapestries, in front of the monumental fireplace decorated with carved foliage.

Anne, aged fifteen and a half, was an attractive girl with fine features framed by beautiful black hair and very slim; she suffered from a slight limp which she passed on to her daughter, Princess Claude. The diplomats considered her wise for her age, quite determined, a girl who knew how to get what she wanted with charm or tears. Brought up in the luxury of the Breton court, she had a great love of fine clothes and, for the ceremony, she wore a dress of gold cloth embroidered with patterns of embossed gold; the sable lining was estimated at 58,000 *livres.* At this time clothes were heirlooms handed down to future generations, folded up in the enormous carved chests which furnished the castles. Of Charles VIII, it could not be said that he was attractive: 'an ugly face with large white eyes and a long, wide aquiline nose; his lips are large which he keeps constantly open' was how the Venetian ambassador described him; but even so Anne fell sufficiently in love with him to be often jealous.

The Bishop of Albi received the couple's consent and the Bishop of Angers said mass. The event was so important that they did not wait for the papal dispensation, necessary because of a distant relationship. The ceremony over, the king conducted his young Breton wife to the residence of Plessis-lès-Tours, near Tours, where the young couple were able to enjoy a standard of comfort and charm still unknown at Langeais.

There is no doubt that the young Anne, having left the austere castles of her duchy could not but admire the beauty of the tapestries and chests assembled in her honour by her husband, as well as the delicate carving on this door into the hall called the Salle du mariage.

Langeais, from the time of Jean Bourré to Jacques Siegfried who bequeathed it to the state and did an admirable job of restoration, has never suffered from additions or suppressions. Here, one can see a small salon decorated with a tapestry of Mille Fleurs *and furnished with carved chests. The woodwork is original, or reconstructed from authentic remains.*

Unfortunately, this Renaissance gem was disfigured in the 18th century. The gallery was bricked up and large windows pierced in the façade, the deep moats were replaced by a terrace and the park was transformed into an English garden! Fashions change and do not repeat themselves. When Dr. Carvalho, who had a passion for archaeology, bought the old residence, he decided to restore its Renaissance style and laid out the garden in a way which would have pleased the Valois kings. With infinite care and love, devo-

In the 16th century the garden was an intellectual reconstruction of nature, an architecture of foliage. In the admirable flower-beds of Villandry, each square in the pleasure garden has a particular shape, evoking different symbols of love.

Villandry and Ussé

One cannot leave Langeais without climbing up to the parapet supported by 270 machicolations, from which a superb view takes in the Loire as far as the confluence with the Indre and Cher which mingle their lazy shining water. One castle after another, like a string of beads, perched on a hilltop or enclosed in a loop of the river. Sometimes the hills retreat from the river bank and give way to a rich alluvial plain irrigated by the tributaries of the Loire.

On the Cher, but a little way off, at the foot of a chalky cliff, Villandry has retained none of its austere past; it was here that Philippe-August and Richard the Lionheart signed their peace treaty. Only a square projecting keep, incorporated into the present day building, remains of the old castle, then called the château de Colombiers. When he bought the property in 1532, Jean Le Breton, secretary to François I, lost no time in building one of those marvellous homes similar to a royal palace but of simpler design: with a main building and two wings framing the main courtyard on three sides; the ground floor arcades forming a gallery and mullioned windows set off by elegant pinnacles.

ting his entire fortune to the project, he remodelled the landscape and created these flowerbeds spreading out in three terraces. What a beautiful picture it makes, these arabesques of clipped box trees, carpets of flowers designed like hooped skirts! From the first terrace there is a view into the distance and a pond reflects the blue sky; on the second, an ornamental garden is composed of clumps of vegetation arranged according to the symbols and allegories of love which were so much appreciated during the Renaissance. On the third terrace, the vegetable garden is like a multicoloured chess-board: vine shoots, trelliswork, fountains and jets of water add a touch of fantasy to the geometry of the surfaces and lines.

Like Villandry, Ussé was built on the site of a medieval fortress, of which only a few fragments remain, and each century was to add to it materials, lines and new styles. But the successive additions, the multitude of roof tops, small belltowers, pinacled sky-lights and chimney stacks create a fairy-like château which so inspired Charles Perrault that he used it as the setting for his Sleeping Beauty. The white stone of the keep is reflected in the Indre and the flower decked terraces form the base: it is like a bouquet of turrets set in a dark forest.

The château changed hands often and belonged to illustrious families, the Bueils, the Princes of Lorraine and Savoie, the Rohan, one of Vauban's daughters, the Duchesse de Duras. Each successfully added his own touch to produce this composite whole where the 15th century façade, still military in style, blends with the three main buildings, gothic to the east, Renaissance to the west and classical to the south. The north wing which blocked the view over the valley, was demolished in the 17th century, while the west main building was extended by a pavilion. There are few examples of a more heterogenous and harmonious combination. On the left of the château, beneath the shade of large cedars, the collegiate church of Ussé rises from a green expanse, built in the 16th century by René d'Espinay. It is one of the attractive Renaissance churches in the Touraine. □

'I had all the clocks stopped so as not to hear the striking of the hours when you would no longer come' wrote the Duchesse de Duras, Lady of Ussé and a new Sleeping Beauty to Châteaubriand; the latter was not indifferent either to the charms of his hostess or to the beauty of the place.

the Indre and the Vienne rivers

The château of Azay-le-Rideau is still a Gothic building with its mullion casements, dormer windows decorated with pinnacles and overhanging turrets; and yet a different atmosphere is created by the poetry of the water and the presence of nature.

LESS GRANDEUR, MORE HARMONY, less majesty and more tenderness: the Indre and Vienne rivers certainly do not possess the majestic fullness of the Loire, but their castles are all the more charming for that.

It has often been said that the Indre is the most delightful river in France, it flows past treasures of architecture such as Azay-le-Rideau, Cormery, Loches, Bridoré and writers have not hesitated to praise it sometimes to excess! Balzac compared the valley to 'a magnificent emerald bowl with the Indre snaking along at the bottom'. A charming, but lazy river: full of twists and turns, sometimes lingering amidst water lilies, sometimes flowing past a mill or hiding in a gloomy copse and although swollen by the water of the Indrois, it joins the Loire slowly, almost reluctantly.

A financier and a business woman

Azay-le-Rideau, like 'a diamond cut into facets', Balzac, once again and this time we are truly in his country — set in an island of greenery, is the great rival on the Indre to Chenonceaux on the Cher. Their destiny was strangely similar, they were both linked with a financier and a business woman. The financier was called Gilles Berthelot: he was master at the Cour des Comptes and Mayor of Tours; he lent money to the crown like his cousin, Semblançay. Through his marriage with the beautiful Philippe Lesbahy, he came into possession of the old fortified building, commonly known as Azay-le-Brûlé. In fact, its name was Azay-le-Rideau, the patronym of a former owner, a knight from Touraine, Ridel or Rideau d'Azay, but, having been burnt down by Charles VIII's troops after a rebellion, the château was given its new name.

However, Berthelot decided to repair the place in 1518 and made it into a residence in keeping with his recent wealth. For eight years his young wife supervised the work which was colossal because of the inconvenience of the site: the river seeped through everywhere and more than a hundred workmen set about drying out the foundations and driving in piles. Two square right angled wings had just been built under the supervision of the beautiful Philippe when a storm broke in the clear sky: Berthelot was implicated in the Semblançay bankruptcy and had to leave in a hurry to avoid finding himself with a rope around his neck. Work was suspended and the château, which should have included four wings set at right angles remains unfinished.

Unfinished for the delight of posterity. Azay is a charming construction, not too imposing and of harmonious proportions: no massive corner towers but gabled turrets, no deep moats but the freshness of the arms of the river. It delights by its discretion, its wide open casements, pilasters and mouldings; a three storeyed loggia in the main building contains an admirable balustraded flight of stairs. The decoration is delicate; the parapets and machicolations are there for ornamentation and the discreetly carved salamander monogram of Queen Claude renders homage to the sovereigns. A vain homage, as the château was not spared; in 1527 it was confiscated as was often the fate of these luxurious homes subject to the power of money and royal desires! François stayed there a few times, long enough to go on a hunt and left the estate to the captain of his guards.

Azay has had a succession of owners. It was bought by the State at the beginning of the 19th century for the sum of 20,000 francs and a Renaissance museum was installed. Its setting amidst foliage and water — the two arms of the Indre were united in the 19th century — have made it one of the most popular châteaux of the Loire, which *son et lumière* spectacles bring back to life every summer. For those who wish to learn about its history in a more amusing and fantastic way, Balzac relates with a gusto worthy of Rabelais in his *Contes drolatiques* 'how the château of Azay was built!'

One of the more modern attractions of Azay-le-Rideau is the monumental staircase with straight banisters, lit by double bays on four floors leading to Italian style loggias.

Like good courtiers, the Berthelot family had the salamander of François I, carved, breathing fire, with the motto nutrisco et extinguo. *Azay is a beautiful example of the efforts made by the state to refurnish the châteaux and bring them back to life.*

The Valley of Lys

Balzac is intimately linked to the beautiful Touraine region. 'If it were not for the Touraine, I would perhaps not be alive' he confessed; it nourished his dreams and strengthened his health, whenever he felt upset or weak he returned there on his doctor's orders.

At Saché, one is filled with nostalgia, not only because, for the hero of *Lys dans la vallée,* the château is 'a melancholy place full of a harmony too serious for superficial people, dear to poets whose souls are broken', but also because the building is still

Balzac was Tourangeau by birth and even more so by feeling: 'Do not ask me why I love Touraine; I love it neither as one loves one's cradle nor as an oasis in a desert; I love it like an artist loves art!'

full of the living presence of the author. It was in this small room, as narrow as a monk's cell — 'the more the soul is physically compressed, the higher it can spring to the heavens' — that he wrote, with the help of endless cups of coffee, some of the most beautiful pages of *La Comédie humaine.* He often forgot the time and the lunch gong made him jump up suddenly. 'They strangled me with their gong', he complained to Mme Carraud! But how he loved them, his longstanding friends, the Margonne family, as a child he used to sit on their knees and they kept an open house for him year after year...

Balzac went there regularly from 1829 to 1837 and he even fell ill, but the view from his window was an immediate consolation, 'with the sky so pure, the oaks so beautiful and the calm so immense'! When he recovered, he walked along the goat tracks beside the banks of the Indre, like his hero Félix de Vandenesse, breathing in the smell of honeysuckle, jasmine and clematis, gleaning from the gentle countryside beneath the hazy sky a detail for a description, a mill standing in the midst of the river, the battered rooftops of a village. In the evening, in the drawing room, he would read some passages from *Lys dans la vallée* to guests, walking up and down and declaiming like an actor.

The valley of the Lys comes to an end at the small village of Pont-de-Ruan or rather Artannes-sur-Indre, at the foot of the church and château. But the vineyards, the ash trees, poplars and birches, the countryside familiar to Balzac continues to follow the river as it meanders up to the square towers of Montbazon. From there, the view is truly beautiful over the mills with their big wheels turning slowly to the rhythm of the water, over sunlit fields sprinkled with towns huddling at the foot of some old fortress mellowed with age: Candé built by the Briçonnet family, where the Duke of Windsor celebrated his marriage, la Tortinière, Vaugrignon, le Puits d'Artigny...

Balzac's table, writing desk, coffee pot, pens, drawings and letters: the entire room, in the château de Saché, is still permeated with his presence.

The Duchesse de Montbazon preferred Couzières — understandably — to the austere family stronghold which dates from Fulk III Nerra. It is a charming manor house with its slated turrets, the shady areas, the terrace, the lawn, the softly gurgling waters of the Indre flowing at the bottom of the park are an incitement to rest and peace: it was here, on a warm September evening, that Louis XIII and his mother, Marie de Medicis, sealed their forced reconciliation in front of hundreds of onlookers from the surrounding countryside hidden in trees and behind shrubs. It provided a setting for idyllic love: here the Duchesse de Montbazon received the gallant visits of the handsome Armand de Rancé, lord of Véretz, who was a neighbour. The death of the young woman, a victim to smallpox, so affected him that he wanted to take away the head of his lovely mistress, clasped to his breast. Unfortunately — a macabre detail — as her body was too long for the coffin, her head had been cut off. At least, that is what legend says; overcome with remorse, Rancé became a Trappist monk.

The Indre captures the waters of little streams; it still washes the ruins of the abbey of Cormery, the old walls of Èvres, some little town hidden behind trees. A tranquil and mild countryside, when all of a sudden at Courçay the valley takes on a romantic appearance, lying between steep rocks as sheer as small cliffs: a sort of Swiss Touraine! But the impression only lasts a minute, after this short burst the Indre slumbers once again amidst pasture lands and regains its fullness thanks to the Indrois.

However modest it may seem, the Indrois, flowing from the Berry, possesses its garland of castles: Montrésor, Genillé, Luzillé... The old fortress of Montrésor, standing upright on a rocky outcrop, was erected by the counts of Anjou, but only two overgrown towers remain of the medieval building. Etymologists have come to the aid of historians and archeologists; according to them, Montrésor means *Mons tres hort,* i.e. 'the three walls', so it must have been a fortified place of some importance during the wars waged by the counts of Anjou; other historians prefer to think that the jewels, silver goblets and gold embossed plates which belonged to Sigismond of Poland, owner of the fortress, gave the château its name: the sad treasures of a defunct monarchy lying behind glass. With its delicate Gothic collegiate church, the lordly dwelling has all the graces of the Renaissance and the village which lies at its foot is one of the most charming in Touraine.

At the confluence of the Indrois and the Olivet an Anjou Count planted a tower on a rocky hill; in the 16th century Imbert de Basternay abandoned this stronghold to build near by this charming Renaissance home, flanked with turrets.

The beautiful Agnès at Loches

Agnès Sorel, the Queen of Beauty, reigned uncontested at Loches. Joan of Arc also spent some time there but the memory of the Maid is overshadowed by that of Agnès, her contemporary, who in her own way gave a decisive impulse to the renovation of the kingdom when she became the king's 'titular' mistress in 1443. The title of royal favourite was completely new in the history of France and destined for a long future.

After Chinon, Loches was the second stronghold owned by Charles VII, the little king of Bourges. It lay right in the heart of the struggles between Capetians and Plantagenets. With its two kilometres of boundary walls, it constituted a notable military unit which rose from a rocky outcrop above the Indre. Beside the old keep of the counts of Anjou, the fortress of Martelet (which dates from the 15th century) rises above several floors of subterranean cells and the Round Tower of Louis XI consolidates the fortification at the exact point where the walls of the city, keep and château join one another, making several angles of fire possible.

Fulk Nerra made Loche into a formidable strong point against the Counts of Blois. Built on the peak of a rocky outcrop, the square keep is surrounded with a powerful enclosing wall, reinforced by the Martelet; the royal entrance can be seen on the flank, but the pyramidal roofs of the collegiate church of Saint Ours, at the far end of the promontory, hide the royal lodgings.

This armour-plated city of stone is entered by a fortified gate situated to the west, while on the other side, the bailey is sufficiently large to house the guard post. The royal château strictly speaking, with its collegiate church of Saint Ours, lies on the opposite side of the fortified dwelling, overlooking the forest and meadows of the Indre valley. Only the old rooms date back to the time of Charles VII; the new ones, more attractive, were built fifty years later for Anne of Brittany. The tower of the beautiful Agnès rises out of the ancient part, but her remains were transferred to the Nouveau Logis: she lies on a slab of white marble set on a black marble base in her ermine surcoat, her feet rest on two lambs and little angels bend over her. So here lies she who showed 'pitiful loving kindness to all men and gave generously, especially to the poor and to the church'. Her remains used to be in the collegiate church, but in 1793 revolutionaries mutilated her statue mistaking it for a saint!

An Angevin style porch protects this admirable romanesque doorway of the collegiate church of Saint Ours; the arches are carved with frightening though delicately polychrome monsters, but the upper section, showing the Virgin and the three kings, is in a very poor condition.

The old, uncomfortable royal lodging was bodly extended along the rocky outcrop by new halls, where this oratory of Anne of Britanny with its fine arcatures is situated; the wall is carved with the ermine tails and girdles which were to become the monograms of widows.

It was perhaps in the house of René d'Anjou at Saumur that Charles VIII met Agnès Sorel. She was to rouse him from his apathy — which Fouquet has so skilfully caught here — and was to manage the government with him.

At Loches, Charles VII, at last free of the English, spent a year of happiness with Agnès. As Fouquet portrays him, with his violet doublet and padded shoulders he is the image of the perfect knight. As for Agnès, she came from a good Touraine family; fair-haired with a high brow, a fine nose, she was 'one of the most beautiful women who lived there then', affirmed the chronicler Olivier de la Marche. And to be convinced one only has to contemplate the marvellous Virgin which Fouquet painted, taking her features for his model.

The king met her when she was lady-in-waiting to Isabelle de Lorraine, the wife of the king of Anjou. He was captivated not only by her beauty but also by her intelligence, for Agnès knew how to surround herself with men of quality. The king showered her with gifts, he presented her with the manor of Beauté-sur-Marne, whose name so aptly applied to her, and other

Here, Agnès Sorel conceals her features: this white marble recumbent figure was mutilated in 1793 and the head of the statue was reconstructed from imagination. But she remains a symbol of flawless beauty, whose whiteness contrasts with the black marble of the tomb.

fiefs in Berry and Normandy. Contrary to custom he treated her like a royal princess: she was even accommodated in the château — his wife, the Queen Marie d'Anjou, lived at Tours or Chinon — and her apartments were decorated with the most beautiful tapestries and hangings. She wore the ornament of royalty, diamonds: the fur-lined trains of her dresses were longer than those of the other ladies.

There is some debate today about the role of Agnès Sorel, and her exact position in regard to Charles VII. Was she an ambitious intriguer or a guardian angel of the kingdom? One chronicler, a Parisian bourgeois, was shocked by her immorality: 'She exposed her shoulders and breasts right down to the nipples'. And the Bishop Jouvenel des Ursins thundered with rage against her extravagance, her indecency and appetite for luxury, he accused her of all the vices, and above all, incitement to debauchery through her influence over the bourgeois ladies, who resemble 'old mules dressed up for market...' No matter how many alms or gifts Agnès distributed, the critics continued to cry out their indignation. They could not forgive her for having upset the traditional image of a woman as discreet and submissive.

There is no doubt that Agnès enjoyed luxury. She was one of the best clients of Jacques Cœur from whom she bought magnificent silks and furs. But she knew how to attract original thinkers, open to new ideas who would contribute to the prosperity of the kingdom. This was her greatest merit; Michelet attributed the salvation of France to her. Vowing an undying — and, according to her most fervent supporters, chaste — love to the king, she followed Charles VII on his travels. She bore him three daughters and was pregnant for the fourth time when her royal lover was waging war in Normandy. She was hastening to join him as soon as possible when she was gripped by excrutiating pains in her stomach at Jumièges, where she had stopped. Poison or dysentry? The young woman was carried off like lightning. Her remains were buried with royal pomp, the heart and entrails interred at Jumièges and the body brought back to the collegiate church of Loches. A few months later the king consoled himself in the company of a niece of the beautiful Agnès.

Loches and its dungeons

With the pacification of the kingdom, a military stronghold such as Loches gradually lost its reason for existing. Rather uncomfortable in spite of improvements, part of the château was converted into a prison. And what a prison! This is where history and legend intertwine and historians disagree: was the cardinal of Angers, La Balue, really locked up in a cage, of only a few cubic meters for several years or not?

La Balue was the son of a tailor from Poitiers who took holy orders. On becoming the king's favourite, he was raised to the position of cardinal and became a member of the Grand Conseil. But as his

The luxuriousness of her gowns, her audacity in laying bare her shoulders and breasts, shocked many contemporaries. Intelligent and beautiful, Agnès Sorel inaugurated the reign of the triumphant woman.

The Indre slowly meanders between woods. To appreciate its charm, one must leave the main roads and learn to rove. Stendhal, in too much of a hurry, only saw 'a flat bank, a miserable little stream'.

favour was beginning to decline, he decided, in 1469, in collusion with the Bishop of Verdun, to launch himself into a double game of politics on the side of the Duke of Burgundy with the intention of offering his services to the king later on as an intermediary. Unfortunately for him, the king's guards surprised one of his emissaries and Louis XI, forewarned, immediately had the two prelates arrested. La Balue was transferred to Montbazon and later locked up in an iron cage in the château of Onzain near Blois, from whence he was transferred to Loches.

The Round Tower at Loches conserved right up to the Revolution two of these famous cages which we know from drawings and descriptions of the 17th century. They had the shape of a cube approximately two metres square, the sides consisted of wooden bars reinforced with iron. A small opening on the side enabled food to be passed to the prisoner and in the rounded door, there was an opening for a basin: this was where the prisoner 'sat to relieve his bowels'. Archive records indicate that the cage could be mounted on joists in order to turn the prisoner round and watch his slightest movements. The cage at Loches was hung five feet above the floor and even today the place where the iron clamps supported it can be seen. As for the 'fillettes', they were heavy linked iron chains by which the prisoner was attached, they were called *fillettes* like *les filles de joie* (women of easy virtue), because the prisoner spent night and day in their company.

Was La Balue a forced guest of the Round Tower? It is not sure as the chroniclers give the names of Onzain, Plessis-lès-Tours and Amboise, but not Loches. In any case, the cages really did exist and had been in use in Italy since the 13th century; Commynes relates that he experienced one for eight months. The account books of the Town Hall at Tours indicate the price of iron fittings, casings and wooden slats.

The Martelet was without possible doubt a sinister prison. Sombre dungeons were installed on several underground floors. This was where rebellious bishops and lords were left to rot, such as the father of Diane de Poitiers and also the famous foreign captive, the Duke of Milan, Ludovico, the Moor taken prisoner at Novara in 1500. This refined Humanist 'at whose court all sorts of subjects were freely discussed even to excess', ended his days in this cell, only a few metres broad, passing his time decorating the walls and ceiling with a myriad of stars to remind him of the heavenly vault. He engraved this moving inscription which is still quite legible: 'I arm myself with patience with the strength of the pain I am made to bear.'

Let us forget the dungeons, the iron cages, and instruments of torture and come out into the sun. Loches is one of the prettiest towns in France with its mosaic of rooftops, its old *hôtels* and little streets. From the royal Residence, delicately designed in the late 15th century, there is a far-reaching view over gardens, fields and green stretches of forest. Agnès loved to leave her castle to gallop along the forest paths or meditate in the abbey of Beaulieu whose beautiful romanesque tower dominates the countryside.

The Indre enters Berry country and flows carelessly between reedy banks and willow clumps; a paradise for contemplative fishermen; it washes the foot of an old tower, a church, a little hamlet reflected in its water and carries the traveller with its lazy rythm to the edge of the province beneath the imposing fortress of Bridoré, gateway to the Touraine. This château was an imposing defensive unit during the Hundred Years War; legend gave it the name of the château of Bluebeard because it was the fief of the feared Gilles de Rais. Today, Bridoré has become a paradise for phlox, gladioli and clumps of bushes which make flashes of green along the ramparts.

Chinon, of great renown

Gentle slopes, vineyards, rich fields through which flow the gentle waters of the Vienne calmer now, after its wild course through the Limousin: this is the country of Descartes and Rabelais, of Saint Martin and Saint Grégoire de Tours. A region of restraint, where none of those picture post-card castles are to be seen, but full of solid, beautiful white homes inhabited by people who appreciate good living, with a hearty laugh, always eager to offer their guests some succulent girdle cake.

The queen of the Vienne is Chinon whose crown of stones dominates the valley. Here a little shepherdess changed the course of history. The fortress, which resembles that of Loches, defended the frontiers of the Angevin empire. Inside this armour of stones, separated by deep moats, stand three mighty châteaux: the projecting fort of Saint Georges, the fort du Milieu and the fort of Coudray built by Philippe Auguste. From the outside the walls display the traditional military arsenal: corner towers, machicolations, barbicans, curtain wall, counterscarp, drawbridge.

Chinon,
four hundred metres in length
and seventy metres wide,
spreads its powerful defensive wall
above the Vienne.
At the eastern point
the Tour de l'Horloge,
built by Philippe Auguste,
serves as an entrance
to the château du Milieu
built in the bailey.
Henry II, king of England,
died here in 1189,
as did his son Richard I ten years later.

A paradise for fishermen,
the Vienne follows its peaceful course
and turns the mill wheels:
the place
seems to have remained the same
for centuries.

This naïve and expressive 15th century tapestry pictures the arrival, in March 1429, of Joan with her little escort beneath the battlemented walls of Chinon; weak and under the influence of his court, Charles hesitated before receiving her.

On Tuesday March 8, 1429, as the setting sun lights up the sky with streaks of red, a dozen archers climb up the steep slope which leads from the town to the château. The little group enters the precinct through a postern gate which leads to the fort of Saint Georges, crosses the drawbridge and, passing through the gothic style gate of the Tour de l'Horloge reaches the château du Milieu, the residence of Charles VII. One of the party, a young girl, has come from Domrémy via Gien and Sainte-Catherine-de-Fierbois: she wears a page's costume, a short grey tunic a black woollen hood and long breeches. Her hair is cut short like a page and she is praying as she mounts the slope. In answer to the sentinel's question, she replies that she wishes to see the king.

Charles VII is hesitant about receiving this strange peasant girl called Joan, who claims to be invested with a message from God. What if she is an English spy? Advisors like La Trémoille scent a plot, an imposture. However, Charles decides to grant an audience but, to test the young girl, he hides amongst his courtiers, dressed like one of them.

The audience takes place in the great hall of the east flank of the royal lodgings, a vast room twenty-seven by nine metres, with three bay windows giving light and access via a small staircase. As night is drawing in, fifty torches are lit, three hundred armed men and lords wait assembled in the hall. The young shepherdess is introduced, she advances fearlessly towards the royal platform, but then turns aside, for the king is not there. Then she pushes her way through the crowd and stops with assurance in front of a rather sickly young man, before whom she bows: 'Sweet Dauphin, my name is Joan the Maid and the Lord of heaven commands you through me, that you shall be consecrated and crowned king in the town of Reims and you shall be the lieutenant to the King of Heaven, King of France.'

An embarrassing situation. Charles, suspicious, gets his clerks to interrogate Joan; then satisfied, he agrees to lodge the Maid in the tower of the château de Coudray. Several discussions take place during the next few days, but they come to nothing. Charles remains suspicious, he sends the brave girl to Poitiers where she undergoes further interrogations. What a waste of time when the valiant Dunois is calling for help! Three weeks pass by, finally on April 20, Charles VII, obliged to find a way out, at last gives the Maid a coat of armour and a small column of soldiers. She leaves immediately along the valley of the Vienne and then the Indre where she makes a brief stay in the old walled city of Azay. She arrives at Tours on April 20 and ten days later she liberates Orléans. Her genuine success has a symbolic implication: hope dawns again. Chinon, a little town of great reputation...

This high mantlepiece between sections of cracked walls is all that remains of the great hall — demolished by order of Richelieu — where Joan of Arc recognized the king; and yet on the soil where the Maid walked, it is easy to conjure up the scene: three hundred armed men lit by torchlight drew aside to let the young girl pass through.

Rue de la Lamproie in Chinon: why bother to point out this little inn bearing a plaque for tourists, amidst all the other picturesque little streets of the old Chinon, lined with timbered houses? This was the home of Antoine Rabelais, lawyer to the royal seat of Chinon, one of the town's important men. His wife gave birth there, in 1493 or 1494, to a baby christened François who in turn gave birth to a giant of literature, Gargantua. According to other traditions, François Rabelais was born five kilometres out of town in a farm owned by his father, situated to the south of the Vienne in the parish of Seuilly, la Devinière.

The old house, of modest proportions, still stands today covered with a slate roof and converted into a museum. One of the rooms on the ground floor is adorned with a monumental mantlepiece. Access to the first floor is up an outside stone stairway protected by a parapet supported by little columns; here was the bedroom of François Rabelais. The house is surrounded by meadows, ploughed fields and vineyards crossed by flowery paths. The works of Rabelais take place here between the path leading to Lerné, the abbey of Seuilly, La Roche-Clermault and the high towers of the château du Coudray-Montpensier including the famous monastery of Fontevrault, which perhaps served as a model for the fantastic abbey of Thélème. One can follow, book in hand, each stage of the terrible war against Picrochole; this war between giants took place in the valley of Négron. Picrochole, defeated, is forced to leave the place, like one leaves an earthly paradise, and flees towards the Ile-Bouchard, gateway to the Touraine.

It is one of those paradoxes of history that the quite modest town of the rabelaisian epic should remain alive for contemporary visitors, full of life and memories, while the sumptuous château of Richelieu near by and the straight-ruled town which borders it are no more than a grave-yard of memories... The château has disappeared, demolished and sold brick by brick... but in the park with its even paths, the statue of Richelieu proudly stands today, host of the surroundings, welcoming visitors. As for the town, it was certainly 'the most beautiful village of the universe', assured La Fontaine, who added mischievously: 'The interior has a few weak points; the main one being that no one lives there!' This strange dead city remains an example of classical urban architecture.

Let us leave the Touraine with one last picture, perhaps the most beautiful, tinged with the holiness of Saint Martin. At the foot of Candes the waters of the Vienne flow into the glistening Loire, the blessed union of two rivers beneath the buttresses of the ancient church. It was here that Saint Martin died: Touraine and Poitiers fought over his remains and, during the night, the monks of Touraine took away the body of the saint with infinite care and transported it by boat down the river to the town of Tours. □

This anonymous portrait of Rabelais wearing his doctor's cap is very expressive: his sensual mouth indicates a love of life, laughter and generosity, but the high forehead and piercing eyes also portray the unflinching clarity of mind and the high standards of the author.

black and white Anjou

Architecturally pure, clear-cut lines, contrast between schist and chalk: the château de Serrant, surrounded by moats, is one of the most beautiful châteaux of Anjou. It was built according to plans drawn by Philibert Delorme, but its construction lasted right until the 18th century.

DU BELLAY WAS RIGHT, the sweetness of Anjou really exists. The province exhales kindness, good nature, sparkling joy which comes from its wine, the perfumed air from the sea, the gaiety of its mills. It charms more than it inspires respect, there is no overpowering monument or crushing countryside. Anjou has a whiff of Italy. The castles, not as pompous as those of the Touraine, are built on a human scale. Many of them having remained in the same family, have conserved their furniture, such as Brissac, Boumois, Montgeoffroy, Serrant and many others. Some stand comparison with the finest royal castles, like Serrant crowned with domes, surrounded by moats, whose curved terraces lead majestically down to the mirror of a vast pond.

It is in Anjou, said Clemenceau, that France is really France; and it may be added that in Anjou France enters Brittany thanks to the Loire. A country of black and white frontiers: the west is already part of Brittany with its granite and black schist harmonizing with the grey sky, heavy with clouds from the sea; to the east, white chalk dominates, sprinkled with vineyards where little towns with slate roofs emerge from a small valley. A country of contrast from one bank to the other: cliffs and steep slopes riddled with troglodyte caves where casks of wine were stored for years, on the left bank face the open plains on the right.

Montsoreau, like a sentinel at the meeting of the Loire and the Vienne, was a strategic point in the Middle Ages. The present château was built by Jean de Chambes, Master of the Royal Hunt, in 1420: it was completely surrounded by water at the time.

The château de Brissac is a good example of unbroken family ownership: here, the bedroom called the Mortemart room — after a maternal grandmother of the Duc de Brissac — is decorated with Louis XIII furniture and classical tapestries showing mythological scenes.

A bloody incident at Montsoreau

Anjou starts at Montsoreau, built above a fishing village in order to survey the route from Poitou and facing Candes in the Touraine. The tower with its spiral staircase, the pilastered decoration, the 15th century façade, the terraced view would suffice to make this charming Renaissance castle famous if an author of genius, Alexandre Dumas, had not already immortalized its name connected with a bloody news item. In reality, the story of *la Dame de Montsoreau* takes place some kilometres away on the other bank at the château de Coutancière.

The lord of Montsoreau, Charles de Chambes, governor of Saumur in 1572, married one of the prettiest women of the Flying Squadron of Catherine de Medicis, Françoise de Méridor, renamed Diane by Alexandre Dumas. The young woman, married in 1576, was presented at court where she caught the attention of one of the favourites of the brother of Henri III, Bussy d'Amboise. As depicted by Dumas, Bussy was a generous, valiant and handsome man, a description which historical records rather contradict; but perhaps Françoise alias Diane saw him through the eyes of the author! Bussy was introduced into the private company of the lady of Montsoreau, he made frequent visits to the château, where the young woman relaxed after court festivities. One day, with typical masculine self satisfaction combined with bad taste, the gallant lover wrote to a friend: 'I have laid a trap for the doe of the great hunter and I have caught her in my net'. The letter fell into the hands of the king's brother, who showed it to Henri III for amusement, and the latter lost no time in transmitting it to the husband. He jumped on his horse and galloped to Coutancière where Diane showed surprise and joy on seeing her dear husband. But Montsoreau was not convinced and forced the said doe to fix a rendez-vous with Bussy by letter. The poor unsuspecting Bussy fell into the trap: on August 18, 1579 he hurried to the château where ten servants, armed to the hilt, awaited him. Bussy made a brave show of defence, but Montsoreau fired the fatal shot. The pistols were still smoking when Françoise flung herself into her husband's arms; they lived happily ever after and had six children.

A sprig of broom on a hat

As might be imagined, Anjou, fief of the fearsome Fulk III Nerra, is covered with castles: and there is not one castle that does not conjure up the memory of the Caesar of Anjou; at least twenty, situated between Anjou and Touraine, of which sometimes not one stone remains, can be attributed to him. To tell the truth, it was his heinous crimes as much as his buildings which made Fulk famous; a greedy, brutal and superstitious man, he embodied all the characteristics of the barons of his age carried to extremes; he expiated rape or assassinations with a gift or a pilgrimage and his repentance was as public as his crimes! In 1870 bones were found in the abbey of Beaulieu which could be his.

A terrible age of war, where violence and piety intermingle. In the 12th century, the counts of Anjou heard the popes appeal to go on crusades and they gave free rein to their brutal appetites by becoming soldiers of God. Geoffroy Plantagenet who wore a sprig of broom in his hat, took up the cross followed by the knights of Anjou. Authori-

Montreuil-Bellay dominates the green valley of the Thouet. Remodelled in the 13th century, enlarged in the 15th, it was restored in the 19th century by a pupil of Viollet-le-Duc who gave free rein to his imagination in his renovation of the gothic façade.

The Abbey of Fontevrault, founded by Robert d'Arbrissel, was open to monks, nuns, widows and repentant girls. An extension of the refectory, the amazing kitchen with its octagonal-shaped cupola giving it a Byzantine air, provided for the needs of the community of 5,000 with its eight hearths.

The four recumbent Plantagenet figures were spared from the havoc of the Revolution; here, in the right transept of the Abbey of Fontevrault one can see Eleanor of Aquitaine and Henry II; just beyond lie the tombs of Richard the Lion Heart and Isabelle of Angoulême. The remains of king John and Henry III were also brought here.

tarian, insolent and passionate, these men were also preoccupied by their salvation, they made donations to abbeys and founded all sort of hospitals, the lazarhouses of La Flèche and Saint-Lazare, the hospital of Saint-Jean at Angers all the while brutally waging war.

Geoffroy retained the warlike spirit of his ancesters and their warcry 'Vallée' resounded over the plains of Anjou. Rebellious vassals should simply keep in their place! Did the lords of du Bellay think themselves invulnerable in the shelter of their massive castles protected by the Thouet river with its deep ravines? Geoffroy neither hesitated about the means nor the time necessary to force them to surrender: he filled in the moats and built towers which his men wheeled along right to the foot of the ramparts, catapults were used to breach the walls, and the soldiers surged through. A siege broke down all further resistance. Taken prisoner, the lord du Bellay was led under strong guard to the fortress of Angers. It required the intervention of the pope and Saint Bernard to obtain his liberation. Conquered and back on their estates, the lords of du Bellay were to die sword in hand, defending their country at Azincourt. As for the château whose towers were partially dismantled, over the course of time, it has taken on its well-known, delightfully disordered appearance, with its old fort, the small 15th century castle which houses a kitchen worthy of Gargantua and the charming Logis neuf with its stairs wide enough for a horse to climb.

Anjou owed to the Plantagenets it short-lived and extraordinary prosperity, traces of which are still visible in this very particular architecture, part romanesque, part gothic which can be seen here and there, on a bridge, in a church, château or market place and is their hallmark. The organization of a powerful state was above all the work of one of Geoffroy's sons, Henri II Plantagenet. The irresistible rise of this vassal to the king of France, took a decisive turn when the council of Beaugency decided to annul the marriage of Louis VII and Aliénor of Aquitaine in 1152. Barely two months later the beautiful Aliénor offered her hand and domain to Henri d'Anjou, ten years her junior. Although Henri was a vassal of the King of France, he did not bother to obtain his consent and did not even present himself when convoked by the court of Capet. More powerful than his sovereign, thanks to his marriage, he reigned over two-thirds of France: Anjou, Normandy, Aquitaine, Maine and Poitou, Auvergne and Touraine. Two years later, in 1154, the hazards of succession made him King of England under the name of Henry II.

The couple received a blessing on their marriage in the magnificent abbey of Fontevrault founded by the preacher Robert d'Arbrissel. The Plantagenets showered the abbey with gifts and it was here, beneath the magnificent Romanesque vaults, that

they chose to rest in eternal peace. The Capetian monarchy made a poor show compared with the splendour of the English kings. But the skill of Philippe Auguste who cleverly enforced claims to sovereigny and bloody family struggles weakened the Plantagenet dynasty. In 1204, encouraging the revolts of vassals and playing on the rivalry between brothers, Philippe Auguste grabbed Anjou from the English. The province was raised to the status of a duchy, then granted by Louis IX to his younger brother Charles, so that from the 13th to the 15th centuries, the Capetian princes, then the Valois family wore the crown of Anjou. However the war was not over: the English and French were to quarrel over supremacy right to the end of the Hundred Years War.

What trials Anjou suffered at that time, a prey to plague, insecurity and war! Fortresses were beseiged like Saumur right in the heart of the fighting; Yolande d'Aragon who settled there made this white citadel above a green valley the centre of resistance. As it stands today, it looks like one of those exquisitely illuminated pages from the *Très Riches Heures du duc de Berry,* with its turrets surmounting old circular towers dating back to Saint Louis. The château was rebuilt or restored several times, fortified in the 16th century, but undoubtedly Yolande d'Aragon found it uncomfortable and preferred to settle in the charming *hôtel* which is traditionally called *hôtel de la Reine de Sicile.* On the other hand, her son René stayed there several times: this flamboyant background, with its small finely sculptured bell towers, its lead roofs ornamented with fine superstructures, *fleurs de lys* and gilded weathervanes which 'glinted when the sun shone on them', this background is clearly made to delight the Good King René, the last sovereign of Anjou before the province was definitively attached to the French crown.

Life was as pleasant at the court of René as at that of his uncle Jean de Berry; and Saumur was quite as good as Mehun-sur-Yèvre! The lord entertained while outside knights competed with one another in tournaments; the combats lasted the whole day.

Louis of Aragon wanted to compete with the splendour of his two brothers, Charles V and Jean de Berry by building on the base of the old fortress of Saumur, this mass of soaring towers, turrets and gables with lead roofs (Miniature from the Très riches Heures du duc de Berry).

René d'Anjou, 'burning desire

René d'Anjou, Comte de Provence, was the author of no great conquest or valiant deed. He was a rather poor politician, lacking money and tenacity. The most adventurous projects crossed his mind. Did he not dream of retaking the kingdom of Naples and reconquering that of Jerusalem? And yet, this dreamer was to bequeath to Anjou a greater gift than that of conquest, a reputation for culture, gentleness and the art of living.

René, an aesthete and epicurean, was an artist in his own right: he devoted himself to illuminating, poetry, theatre; he wrote *le Livre du cœur d'amour épris* and, through festivities and pageants he attempted to revive the chivalric ideal with its ceremony and refinement; drums, minstrels, Moorish slaves dressed in Saracen costumes and turbans, exotic animals, jokers and fools, monkeys dressed in satin all gave his court a sumptuous air of the East; his courtiers wore magnificent costumes and he himself was dressed like a Turk in a tunic of gold cloth embroidered with arabic letters. Above all, René who created the Knighthood of the Crescent Moon, enjoyed organizing jousts and tournaments in which the most handsome of his suite took part. The jousting at Saumur for the arrival of his second wife, Jeanne de Laval, lasted forty days, punctuated with dramatic spectacles and *tableaux vivants.* The horses pranced, the lords donned their finest armour and trumpets blew fanfares; René was dressed in black armour and seated on a horse decked out in a black cape, he won the prize for the *joute du pas.*

This man, who seemed to place so much importance on appearances, was a pas-

The octagonal towers are all that remain of the château of Louis d'Anjou; René, his grandson, undertook the restoration of the east tower or chapel tower, and he replaced the lead roofing with slate tiles.

sionate lover of nature which made him modern in outlook and close to us: he often left his immense fortresses to live in country retreats, those little manor houses which he built near Saumur or Angers: Launay, Chanzé, Beaufort, Baugé, les Rivettes, Reculée, hunting lodges in the forest of Baugeois, small enclosed estates or residences amidst vineyard. He took part in the drawing up of plans; at Reculée, he most probably decorated the *Chambre aux Groseilles rouges* and the *Galerie aux Chaufferettes* which is decorated with his motto: 'Burning desire'. 'He took recreation', noted a chronicler, 'and modest pleasure in planting, grafting trees, building arbours, pavilions, orchards, having ditches dug and deepened, fish ponds and pools to feed his fish, rearing birds of different species in order to delight in their song'. What a time-table for a country gentleman before his time!

To take delight and make merry while watching the gentle Loire flow by... Saumur was to remember this golden age when she was once again in the midst of combats, a Protestant city torn by the terrible Wars of Religion, where the governor Montsoreau, on the king's orders, organized a Saint Bartholomew massacre of the Huguenots at the end of August 1572. However, hommage is still rendered today to the jousts and pageants of the 15th century when the cadets of the *Ecole de cavalerie* of Saumur go through their dazzling exhibitions, tilting the ring, fantasias, passage at arms; every year the equestrian tilting matches of the *Cadre noir* draw thousands of spectators, who probably know nothing of the 'pas de Saumur' of the Good King René...

A few kilometres away, almost on the outskirts of Saumur, the little town of Dampierre, perched on chalky slopes, a region of cabernet cultivators and mushroom growers, spreads out its houses above the Loire. A rather dilapidated manor house with two square towers barely attracts attention: it is the château des Morains. Here the daughter of René d'Anjou, the little Princess Marguerite, spent her childhood. She was beautiful, intelligent but unfortunately poor: many suitors turned aside because the king was unable to provide her with a sufficient dowry. History relates that one of her childhood companions was a young boy from Dampierre, son of the lord of La Vignolle and she probably would have chosen him for husband if she had not pleased the young king of England, Henry VI. At fifteen, the young Marguerite was sent as a wife—or a hostage?—over the Channel to seal the reconciliation between the two countries. But things did not turn out well for Marguerite, passionate and uncontrollable, who arrived right in the middle of the Wars of the Roses. After years of battles, captivity and mourning she finally returned to France, where Louis XI offered her his protection in exchange for Anjou and Touraine. Repatriated, the admirable Marguerite took care of her good town of Saumur and died

in 1482, aged fifty-three, in the château des Morains, attended by her faithful La Vignolle.

Apocalypse at Angers

How beautiful the Loire is between Saumur and Ponts-de-Cé! Islands with golden banks float like a chain and cut the river into several streams; almost all the towns and villages are little ports where watermen can find rings set in the stone to tie up their barges. On the banks, fishermen's nets dry in the sun and the diving flight of gulls reminds us of the closeness of the sea. The Loire widens out to join the ocean, full of sails like 'those women of a certain age who know how to love with a love matured and swollen with the tributaries of life', this was how Balzac saw Ponts-de-Cé.

Ponts-de-Cé, the 'Seium' of the Romans, built over three islands linked by arches, constitutes the suburbs of Angers. René d'Anjou loved to retire to a pavilion which he had built on his estate, from where he enjoyed watching on Ascension Day after vespers, the *baillée des filles,* a sort of contest between young girls aged eighteen: the one who caught the most fish in record time presented her catch to the king who kissed her and gave her a dowry. The same evening, fish was eaten with local wine; the good king himself took great delight in fishing and he was called the king of the roach!

What a contrast between these agreeable scenes and the dark château d'Angers on the Maine! No sweetness without force. With its seventeen towers, stripped of their pin-

In a few years, Saint Louis had this colossal enclosing wall built, measuring 960 metres in length, flanked by seventeen towers facing the west, the weak spot in its defence, and eighty metres high. Cut down to the level of the curtain wall, they retain a feeling of strength which contrasts with the gothic fragility of the chapel.

This 15th century tapestry gives an accurate picture of elegant rides on horseback in the forests and countryside. They were as much a part of the life of the châteaux as were the delights of hunting.

nacles in 1589, streaked with grey schist, blind walls and dark slate, its old ditches which the river Maine used to fill, the château scarcely conjures up the proverbial sweetness of Anjou; its wild grandeur is more reminiscent of Fulk Nerra, who flung his wife Elizabeth from the ramparts, convinced of her adultery. Over the centuries, the fortress was a disputed stake between Bretons and Romans, then the English and the French, between the Huguenots and *Ligueurs* and finally, between Vendeans and Revolutionaries: the old dilapidated towers bear the scars of war.

However, a gem of a chapel erected by Yolande d'Aragon and the magnificent tapestries of the Apocalypse may give some idea of the past splendour. It was Louis I d'Anjou, a great traveller, with a taste for luxury, who ordered these famous tapestries. The prince liked to dazzle; he had expensive furs sent from Brussels, clothes embroidered with gold and pearls, of which his accounts reveal the cost. The execution of the tapestries, finished around 1385, took years because of their size: one hundred and sixty-eight metres long, five metres high, divided into seven pieces of equal length; a synthesis of all the art of the age, which were to brighten the walls of the old château with their colours of light red and blue. The grandson of Louis d'Anjou, King René, bequeathed the masterpiece to the cathedral of Saint Maurice, while the tapestry-makers of the Loire set to work once again to decorate the walls of the fortress in the spirit of the age: these are the tapestry of a Thousand Flowers with its warm colours, each petal requiring months of work! Spring comes sooner...

In spite of the grim aspect of its castle, Angers is not a sad town: perhaps it owes its gaiety to the generations of students who have followed one another since the 13th century. Even the ruins of the château inspire more emotion and poetry than many other over-restored homes: these large circular towers, worn by time, resemble pebbles polished by the sea and, indeed, as Flaubert so prettily said 'history is like the sea, beautiful because it effaces'.

The angel of the Apocalypse can demolish all walls, even those of Angers! A river of blood flows from a cask of grapes. These magnificent tapestries depicted 98 scenes, spread over seven large rooms alternatively red and blue.

The Loir, the pride of Vendômois

Tourist circuits often injustly avoid the Loir. However, this little river, as lazy and weedy as the Indre, is the 'pride of the Vendômois' as Du Bellay said; and Racan also paid hommage to its peaceful valley, 'where my rest begins, where my torment ceases'. From the Ile-de-France to Anjou, the Loir flows parallel to the Loire, like a modest vassal following his lord and receiving the crumbs of his greatness.

The château du Verger in Anjou was the proud abode of Pierre de Rohan, Maréchal de Gié, from 1482; it is a château worthy of the Valois kings with its six circular towers, its double line of moats, gallery for feasts, parapet walk, avenues, kennels and ponds; Charles VIII signed a peace treaty there with the Duke of Brittany and Pierre de Rohan was so favourable to the attachment of the duchy to France that he barred the route when Anne of Brittany decided to return to Nantes: an imprudent gesture which resulted in his exile. Alas, of these past splendours, only a few fragments remain, the immense silex towers, crowned with machicolations in white chalk.

It is better to look for signs of this magnificence at Durtal. The view which embraces the river and château is marvellous. The residence belonged to a close friend of the Valois kings, François de Scepeaux, Maréchal de Vieilleville. In this carved gem of the 15th and 16th centuries, all the pleasures found in the Val de Loire are available: riding parties in the neighbouring forest of Chambiers, hunts, fine banquets, magnificent receptions were held here as well as at château du Verger. Henri III went there in 1550; Charles IX spent a whole month with Queen Catherine de Medicis; the Maréchal honoured them with a hunt and on their return they both 'drank the green and the dry' relates the chronicler.

The luxury of the reception given by Catherine de Medicis when she received the Polish ambassadors, makes it easy for us to imagine the incredible preparations necessary when a lord had the honour of entertaining the queen!

Châteaudun seems to lie outside the rumours of hystory; the château dominates the Loir, this 'silver spring' where Ronsard so often came to dream.

From La Flèche, a studious little enclave whose Jesuit college took in such famous pupils as Descartes and Mersennes, to the château du Lude, the Loir flows slowly in a barely undulating countryside full of quiet grace. One crosses wide meadows planted with fruit trees, fields of maize, cultivated fields: who could believe that this was where the English and French tore one another to pieces during the Hundred Years War? Here and there lie the remains of a rampart or tower topped by a watch-turret whose slate roof emerges from the trees, but the countryside breathes serenity. The four great towers of Lude do not inspire fear either: the feudal castle was transformed into a mansion in the 15th century by the lord of Daillon, a comrade of Louis XI, who named him Jehan des Habiletés. Like master, like servant. The work lasted several years, it was still not finished under Louis XII to whom the Daillon family rendered homage, as good servants, by carving the porcupine. The château de Lude reminds one a little of Chaumont: the parapet walk decorated with sculptures was used as a promenade and the flowery ornamentation, the pedimented dormer windows are merely decorative. The François I wing adorned with pilasters and medallions overlooks a very beautiful park which stretches down to the Loir and which was adorned in the 17th century with numerous statues and marble vases. The inside of the château beneath the protection of family portraits, still offers the intimacy of lived in homes: the reception hall houses the rehearsals of the entertainments at Lude.

Once past Lude, the banks of the Loir become more uneven. Chalk cliffs house troglodyte dwellings hidden behind wild bushes and climbing plants. At Château-du-Loir it is not a château you must look for—the fortress has been destroyed—but at the foot of a charming church the memory of Ronsard. In 1560, the clerk, Pierre de Ronsard, received the archdeaconry of Château-du-Loir, and a prebend as canon of the cathedral. It was enough to assure him a livelihood and enable him to devote himself to meditation and poetry. He wrote delicate verses to a young peasant girl from Bourgueil, Marie Dupin, and in order to see her, he is prepared to abandon the court and the king! His Muse remained a country girl and his message, 'Gather ye rosebuds while you may', was designed

The Loire bathes the gardens of the château du Lude. Jehan de Daillon used the master workmen of King René to built this beautiful country retreat in the Sarthe which was enlarged and renovated in the 18th century.

to please the amiable society of the Valois. Four years later, Ronsard received the priory of Saint-Cosme-en-l'Isle.

A few kilometres from Château-du-Loir, a white country mansion backs onto the edge of the forest of Gastine: La Possonnière. The exterior façade is modest and the life of the house is turned towards the inner courtyard. It is within these walls that Pierre de Ronsard was born in 1524; the child grew up in ideal surroundings to awaken his vocation: his father Loys was a man much taken with Humanism; when he returned from the Italian wars, he restored his residence according to the fashion of the day and embellished it with numerous Latin and French inscriptions, during his leisure or rather the long captivity, which he suffered in Spain when accompanying the sons of François I, he composed a treaty in verse. His motto inscribed over the doorway, 'To pleasure and grace', could not but inspire the young Pierre, whose greatest delight is to dream on the banks of the river 'lying flat' in the shade of the Green Island, at the point where the waters divide into several streams: these youthful impressions never grew dim. In the neighbouring little church of Couture, rest the parents of the poet, while Ronsard himself is interred at Saint-Cosme.

Still more fields, and here is Troo, a quaint village full of troglodyte dwellings from which cracked sections of the old fortified walls emerge. The châteaux continue to file past, some (such as Lavardin overlook a ravine) have retained their proud appearance: the lords of Lavardin bravely resisted the attacks of Richard the Lionheart. The Loir twists again before reaching Vendôme; it bathes the château of the Bourbons on a ford over the Loir—good fortune at the ford, as the song goes! At Vendôme, the little river is no longer part of Touraine, but belongs to the Beauce and it returns to the home of the counts of Vendôme. Another region appears.

How many châteaux of the Loire are there? Two hundred? Two hundred and fifty? Even more, if one adds to the historical residences the old mansions, priories and manors. Nestling in a valley or crowning a hill, on the edge of a forest or in the bend of the river, they stand as witnesses to the continuity of history, and the local white stone often gives them an air of eternal beauty. Some of them, of course, are no more than superb ruins overgrown with weeds and bushes, but others seem so intact that, like Flaubert, one can almost hear 'the laughter of pages and the rustle of long trains'. The Loire has sensibly silted up, beautiful and useless, she thus preserves the charm of her banks. It is still good to live here even though encroaching concrete may threaten. The evening light of Touraine, the whiteness of the stone, chalk slopes, the birch trees and poplars which shiver in the warm winds... 'I have memories of towns as one has memories of love' said Valery Larbaud; let us parody him and may you have memories of châteaux, as you have memories of love... □

Ronsard composed La Franciade *in the priory of Saint Cosme on the Loire, not far from Tours. In the nearby garden he cultivated melons. He spent the last days of his life in this room, he even composed two sonnets on the eve of his death.*

Amboise, *5,* 25, 82, *83, 84, 85;*
Angers, 18, *135;*
Azay-le-Rideau, *112-113, 114;*
Baugé, 134;
Beaufort, 134;
Beaugency, 19, 28, *34;*
Beauregard, *70;*
Béchellerie (la), 103;
Blois, *21, 24,* 25, 36, *37, 40-41, 42-43, 46-47, 49, 50-51;*
Boumois, 128;
Bourdaisière (la), 69;
Bridoré, 112, 121;
Brissac, 31, 76, *128;*
Candé, 115;
Chambord, 24, 25, *54-55, 56, 57, 58, 62-63, 66-67;*
Chanteloup, 91;
Chanzé, 21, 134;
Châteauneuf-sur-Loire, 28, *31,* 32;
Chaumont, *19, 80-81, 82;*
Chenonceaux, *92-93, 96-97, 98-99;*
Cheverny, *25,* 31, *73, 74-75;*
Chinon, 18, *122-123, 125;*
Cinq-Mars, 106;
Clos-Lucé (le), *89;*
Cormery, 112;
Coudray-Montpensier (le), 21;
Coutancière, 129;
Couzières, 116;
Devinière (la), 126;
Durtal, 138;
Fontevrault, *130-131;*
Fougères-sur-Bièvre, *19;*
Genillé, 116;
Gien, *26-27, 28;*
Grenadière (la), 103;
Gué-Péan, 101;
Herbault, 21, 69;
Jargeau, 28;
Langeais, 19, 21, *22-23, 108-109;*
Launay, 21, 134;
Lavardin, 141;
Loches, 18, 112, *117, 118;*
Lude (Le), *140;*
Luynes, 21, 31, 76, *106-107;*
Luzillé, 116;
Mehun-sur-Yèvre, *18;*
Menars, 25, 76, *77-78;*
Meung-sur-Loire, 28, 32, 34, 35;
Montbazon, 19, 115;
Montgeoffroy, 128;
Montrésor, *116;*
Montreuil-Bellay, 21, *130;*
Montrichard, 19, 101;
Montsoreau, *129;*
Morains (les), 134;
Morinière (la), 25, 72;
Moulin de Lassay (le), *20,* 21, *71;*
Nançay, 21;
Noisay, 91;
Onzain, 121;
Orléans, *12,* 18, 28;
Plessis-Bourré (le), *16-17,* 21;
Plessis-lès-Tours, 21, *104, 105;*
Poncé-sur-le-Loir, 25;
Possonnière (la), 141;
Puits d'Artigny (le), 115;
Reculée, 21, 134;
Richelieu, 126;
Rivettes (les), 134;
Saché, *115;*
St-Aignan, *24,* 101;
St-Benoît-sur-Loire, *32-33;*
Saumur, *132, 133;*
Selles-sur-Cher, 101;
Serrant, *127;*
Sully-sur-Loire, 28, *29, 30, 76;*
Talcy, *72;*
Tortinière (la), 115;
Tours, 18, *102-103;*
Ussé, *110-111;*
Valençay, *101;*
Vaugrignon, 115;
Vendôme, 141;
Verger (le), 21, 138;
Villandry, *11,* 69, *110;*
Villesavin, 25, *69;*

Iconographic notes

6, *16th century Flemish tapestry, Museo dei Uffizi, Florence;* ***12,*** *19th century engraving;* ***14,*** *late-15th century tapestry from the Netherlands, musée de Cluny, Paris;* ***15,*** *miniature from the collection,* les Chants royaux, *1502, Bibliothèque nationale, Paris;* ***18,*** Très Riches Heures du duc de Berry, *musée Condé, Chantilly;* ***29,*** *portrait by François Quesnel, musée Condé, Chantilly;* ***31,*** *private collection;* ***35,*** *Bibliothèque nationale, Paris;* ***38,*** *mid-15th century tapestry from Arras, musée des Arts décoratifs, Paris;* ***39,*** *first edition by Pierre Levet;* ***40,*** *painted wood panel, Bibliothèque nationale, Paris;* ***44,*** *wash tint and drawing by Antoine Caron, Louvre;* ***45,*** *anonymous portrait, late-16th century, musée Condé, Chantilly;* ***46,*** *19th century engraving;* ***48,*** *red chalk drawing by François Clouet, musée Condé, Chantilly;* ***52,*** *engraving by François Hogenberg, Bibliothèque nationale, Paris;* ***53,*** *anonymous 17th century painting, musée de Blois;* ***59,*** *water-colour on parchment, musée Condé, Chantilly;* ***60-61,*** *tapestry,* François Ier à la chasse, *salle des Chasses, château de Chambord;* ***62,*** *Clouet School, musée Condé, Chantilly;* ***62-63,*** la Chasse de Louis XIV *by Van der Meulen, château de Versailles;* ***65,*** *pastel, Louvre;* ***66-67,*** *19th century engraving;* ***77,*** *Rothschild collection;* ***82,*** *château de Chenonceaux;* ***86-87,*** *diptych, anonymous painting, Grand Salon, château de Langeais;* ***88,*** *self-portrait, red chalk, Academia, Venise;* ***90,*** *Bibliothèque nationale, Paris;* ***94,*** *anonymous painting, château de Chaumont;* ***95,*** *anonymous painting, Museo dei Uffizi, Florence;* ***100,*** *anonymous painting, musée des Beaux-Arts, Rennes;* ***102-103,*** view of Tours in 1797 *by Charles-Antoine Rougeot, musée des Beaux-Arts, Tours;* ***104,*** *water-colour, 1699, Bibliothèque nationale, Paris;* ***105,*** *Brooklyn Museum, New York;* ***107,*** *Le Nain School, musée d'Art et de Céramique, Narbonne;* ***115,*** *pastel drawing of Balzac aged 40, musée des Beaux-Arts, Tours;* ***119,*** *portrait after the French School, c. 1480, Louvre;* ***120,*** *anonymous painting, private collection;* ***124,*** *Musée archéologique, Orléans;* ***126,*** *anonymous 17th century painting, château de Versailles;* ***132,*** Très Riches Heures du duc de Berry, *musée Condé, Chantilly;* ***133,*** Très Riches Heures du duc de Berry, *musée Condé, Chantilly;* ***134,*** la Galante Chevauchée, *tapestry from the workshops of Arras, c. 1450, château de Saumur;* ***136-137,*** *tapestry of the* Apocalypse *by the warper Nicolas Bataille, château d'Angers;* ***138-139,*** *16th century tapestry, Museo dei Uffizi, Florence.*

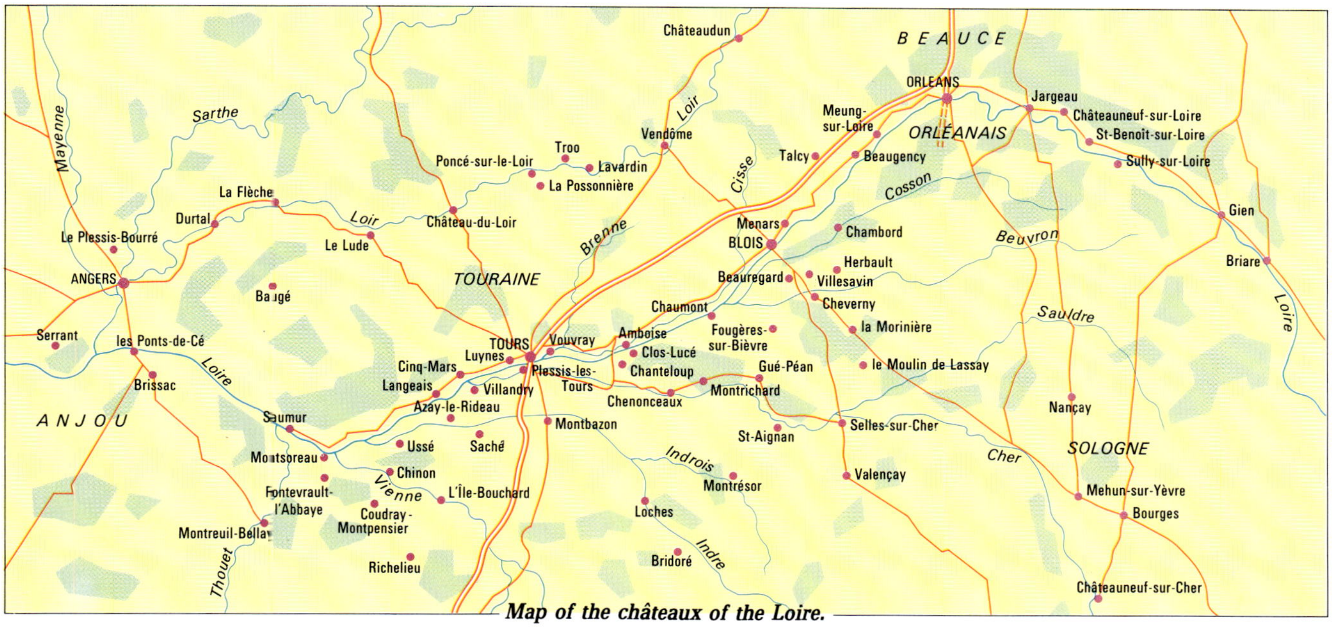

Map of the châteaux of the Loire.

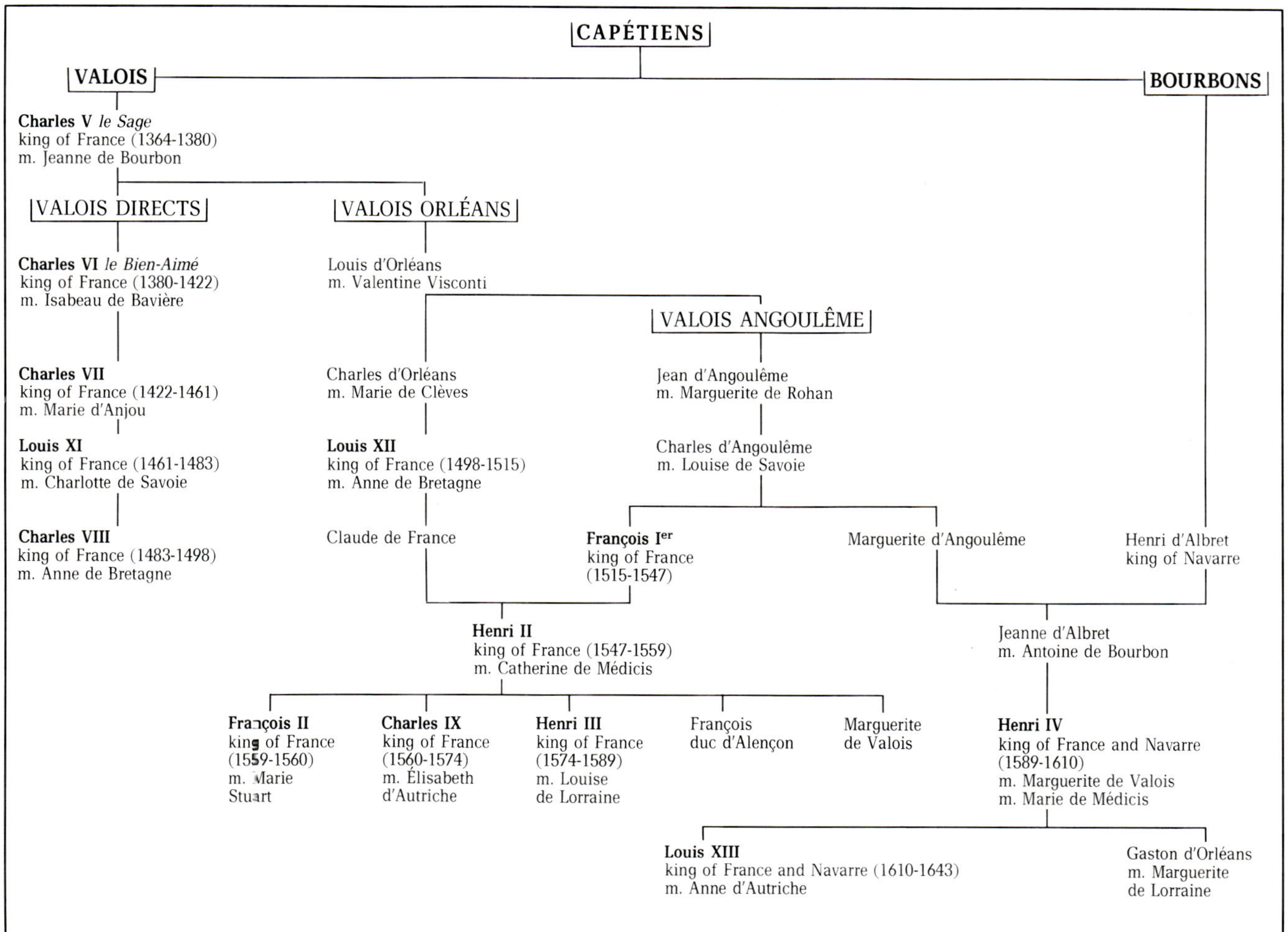

Simplified genealogy of the Valois

Photographic credits

F.-X. Lovat-Atlas-Photo, **26-27;** Bibliothèque nationale, **35, 40** (below); Jean Bottin, **11** (below), **31** (below); Brooklyn Museum of New York, **105** (below); Claude Rives-Cedri, **27, 69;** Gérard Sinoen-Cedri, **11** (centre on the right), **92-93, 106-107, 121, 122-123** (2), **127, 128, 129, 133** (above on the right), **138** (below); B. and C. Desjeux, **29** (below), **130** (on the left), **140;** G. Sommer-Explorer, **21;** Giraudon, **18, 48, 62** (below on the left), **90, 126, 132, 133** (below on the left); Anderson-Giraudon, **88;** Lauros-Giraudon, **14, 29** (above), **31** (below), **38, 39, 44, 45, 52, 53, 59, 65, 100** (above), **107** (above on the right), **120, 130-131** (below); Lauros-Giraudon-Ségalat, **15;** Telarci-Giraudon, **77;** F. Jalain, **13;** Pix, **7** (above and below), **10, 12, 19** (below), **22-23, 28, 32-33, 34, 40-41** (3 above), **42-43, 46** (2), **47, 49, 50-51** (2), **57, 58** (below on the right), **62-63, 66-67, 74-75, 78, 80-81, 82** (below on the left), **82-83, 84, 85** (2), **86-87, 89, 94** (2), **95, 96-97** (2), **108** (above), **110-111** (2), **114** (2), **118** (2), **119** (2), **125, 131** (centre on the right), **134, 136-137;** Bénazet-Pix, **7** (centre), **102-103, 115** (2), **141;** J.-C. Charmet-Pix, **104, 124;** Delon-Pix, **70** (above on the right); Gontscharoff-Pix, **36-37;** Richard List-Pix, **56;** Revault-Pix, **60-61;** B. Beaujard-Rapho, **37;** Serraillier-Rapho, **25;** Rozencwajg, **67, 117;** Scala, **138-139;** Scala-Ziolo, **6** (below); Michel Guillard-Scope, **5, 8-9, 58** (above on the left), **68-69, 92, 135;** Rosine Mazin-Top, **6** (above), **16, 17, 19** (above), **20, 24** (2), **30, 54-55, 69, 72, 73, 98-99, 100-101** (below), **105** (above), **108** (below), **109, 112-113, 116.**

Photocomposition M.C.P., Fleury-les-Aubrais.

Photogravure et Impression HERACLIO FOURNIER, VITORIA. – Dépôt légal : avril 1984.
N° série Éditeur 12096. – IMPRIMÉ EN ESPAGNE. *(Printed in Spain)*. – 523106-Avril 1984.